9788496954786

RGB

Reviewing Graphics in Britain
Edited by Marc Valli and Richard Brereton

004/288

009–287

Three types of designers you will find at The Three Kings
by Marc Valli

The first question one has to ask is: but is there such a thing as British graphics? What can legitimately be called British, and what cannot? Tricky question. Contemporary Britain is unmistakably cosmopolitan. A selection criteria based purely on nationality, on passports, would not do the trick. Even the idea of focussing on practitioners who reside in the UK was problematic: in the age of broadband, designers can move freely around the world, while continuing to work for British clients and within a British sphere. We therefore decided to use the looser, trickier idea of 'belonging', or 'fellowship', constantly asking the question: how does this work fit into the UK's visual art scene? But that brings us back to our starting point: what is that then? Is there such a thing as British graphics?

In my view the answer to this question is, typically, yes and, well, no... Yes, in the sense that there is work that manifestly belongs to this culture, and no in the sense that in the UK today there doesn't appear to be one predominant style. Moreover, the diversity of styles and influences is clearly one of the key characteristics of the graphics produced in this country. In fact, on this tour of contemporary British graphics, three distinct characteristics did stand out for me, and I have come to believe that they correspond to the three main facets of the British graphic design scene.

The first thing that did strike me was the astonishingly high level of stylistic sophistication and erudition of the work in front of me. I am thinking, for example, about the work of Mark Farrow, Browns, Bibliothèque, Studio8, Sea, North, Mike & Rebecca, Dan Eatock, Design Project, Spin, MadeThought, Multistorey, NB Studio, Proud Collective, Shaz Madani, William Hall and Angus Hyland at Pentagram. As I write this list down, I can't avoid noticing that London-based practitioners are prevalent. In fact, all except one of those mentioned above are based in London, though it must also be noted that a significant proportion of them are not from London. But if you are a design practitioner in the UK, London is somehow inevitable. Even if your studio is not based in the capital, you are likely to still come regularly down on the train in order to attend meetings, exhibitions, conferences. Not all ambitious British designers choose to establish themselves in London, but a lot of them do. These sophisticated London dwellers produce concept-led and incredibly well-informed work. I believe this style is, to some degree, the product of this particular milieu, which has plenty to offer in terms of influence and inspiration, without imposing many constraints on individual creatives. More than anywhere else in the world, British graphic designers have been free to roam through design history, developing visual styles without the pressure of a dominant, overarching stylistic or theoretical framework. Like barbarian hordes entering more civilised but less dynamic territories, these young raiders were able to absorb influences such as the Swiss International Style and the Dutch, American and various other forms of modernism, and transform them into a vibrant new form. As a reaction to the abundance of material around them, these new converts operate, for a majority of the time, within a rather strict minimalist aesthetic. They have resisted a general tendency to abuse new image making software and create flashy and facile images, preferring instead to stick to the basics of graphic composition and type layout.

Nevertheless, true to their modernist calling, they also make sure that the results look absolutely and radically contemporary, not hesitating to splash on specials and colours and textures, or throw a spontaneous gesture or post-modern twist into the mix. Being able to service a cosmopolitan, sophisticated and non-traditionalist clientèle has certainly also been a factor in the development of this particular style. Over the years, it has produced disciplined, timeless and disconcertingly stylish designs for this well-off clientèle, while giving the UK's arts & culture sectors a very recognizable look.

The second characteristic of UK-based graphic design seems, initially at least, diametrically opposed to the first one. From concept-led design, we do a U-turn to move towards highly illustrative, image-led work – in other words, from design work to graphic work. Relentless visual experimentation has been a trademark of British graphics. The heirs of Vaughn Oliver & V23 have continued to refuse easy, pleasing, carefully ordered imagery in order to search for new ways of making images – unique and previously unimaginable images. When saying this, I am thinking about the likes of The Designers Republic (TDR), Build (Michael Place, ex-TDR), Universal Everything (Matt Pyke, also ex -TDR), Ehquestionmark, Graphic Thought Facility (GTF), Accept & Proceed, Julian House (Intro), Family, Hellovon, Tom Hingston, Me Company, Airside, Studio Tonne, Rick Myers, Attik, James Joyce (One Fine Day), Studio Output, and Jonathan Barnbrook. We're still often in London here, but also in Manchester, Sheffield, Birmingham, Brighton, Huddersfield, Nottingham… The balance has shifted, away from London, and the prying and judgemental eyes of fellow designers, towards the unquiet North and other less over-designed corners of the UK.

In particular, these designers have supplied the UK's phenomenally successful and productive music industry with visuals. Record labels (such as Factory Records, 4AD, Warp, Ninja Tunes and Lex) proved to be accommodating patrons, allowing designers to let rip – which they did, going at visuals with both a vision and a vengeance. They have explored 3D imagery and architectural photography, all kinds of digital illustration, ornamentation, graffiti, chemistry charts, origami techniques… They have obliterated type, pulled down grids, rejected symmetry, distorted scale, warped perspective, scrambled language… They have used stains, holes, hairs, marker pens, Stanley knives… They have defaced covers, subverted signage systems and even, in one case, studied disinterred medieval graves and torture instruments, in their quest for striking and strikingly new images and visual styles. Lively? Hell, yes…

The final characteristic I would like to mention (or come back to) in relationship to graphic design in the UK is its eclecticism. Here I am thinking about hopelessly cosmopolitan figures such as Fernando Gutiérrez, Fuel, Non-Format, Åbäke, FI@33, Vince Frost, Domenic Lippa (Pentagram), Alex Rich, Tomato. Not to mention the Pentagram umbrella, which, despite its strict rules and high standards and demands, ends up functioning as a sanctuary for elegantly eclectic styles. The focus has shifted again, this time not just away from London, but from the UK altogether. Post-colonial Britain is a vast melting-pot of cultures. The UK's economy, and in particular its design, advertising, art and fashion industries could not survive without foreign markets, foreign capital and foreign labour. English, being the ultimate international language in a globalised world, continues to act as a magnet for business and talent. Every year, thousands of ambitious art students from all over the world enrol into British art courses. As they pay higher fees, these foreign students are welcomed with open arms by British schools. They are also welcomed by prospective employers afterwards. Nowadays, you can hardly find a studio in London which does not employ at least one foreign designer, even if simply as work experience. Horizons have broadened, connections were made and kept, and tastes, habits and practices changed significantly in the process.

Of course, dividing designers into categories is a flawed strategy: fun for geeks, on a level with top ten movies or musical genres. In truth, the majority of the designers mentioned above can boast of at least two, if not all three, of these characteristics. And none more so than Peter Saville. Not included in the present book for reasons we shall outline below*, Saville possesses all the three main attributes of British graphic design – refinement, visual innovation, eclecticism – in abundance, and the unique combination of these have made him one of the greatest image makers of his time. In decades to come, we may look back upon the work of British graphic designers and realise that Saville is not the only one who fits that description.

There is one last observation I would like to make. In the last decade, new technologies have allowed small studios to take on bigger jobs. We have witnessed a move away from the big corporate studios of the nineties and towards smaller and more flexible set-ups, not dissimilar from those which allowed seminal artists such as Alan Fletcher (Pentagram), Barney Bubbles, Peter Saville, Malcolm Garrett, Jamie Reid, Terry Jones, Vaughn Oliver (V23), Neville Brody, Sean Perkins (North) and Ian Anderson (TDR) to create some of the most stunning and influential visuals of the seventies, eighties and nineties. May this new wave of raiders be able to carry this spirit of innovation, refinement, experimentation and individuality deep into this yet to be shaped century.

* PS I

The main problem when compiling this book has been the over-abundance of relevant material and important names. People will inevitably feel frustrated (if not indeed aggravated) by our selection. A book such as this one is bound to be noted for the names it leaves out more than for those it includes. So I thought it would be useful to say a few more words about our selection criteria. Firstly, we tried to focus on the last five to ten years, leaving the eighties and the nineties behind. This is why still fully active luminaries such as Peter Saville, Malcolm Garrett, Terry Jones, Neville Brody, Sean Perkins (North) and Ian Anderson (TDR) are not included here. That was the easy part. After that, everything became subjective and debatable. We felt some people may have been overrepresented in print and decided to leave them out. We also felt, for example, that Fernando Gutiérrez had too much 'Spain' in his work and decided, much to our regret, to leave him out. At the end of the day, our main preoccupation in making this selection was to put into evidence the quality, the richness and the diversity of the graphic work being produced in and around this island.

* PS 2

If you are disappointed by the fact that we have not provided photographs of the designers featured in the book, or if you would like to know more about them and the British graphic design scene in general, you could do worse than go for a drink at the lovely Three Kings pub in Clerkenwell Green (opposite the entrance of the church). The Guinness is good and you will sometimes find fellow graphic designers working behind the bar. I wouldn't be surprised if quite a few of the designs featured in this book had been drunkenly dreamt up around its tables, or on the steps leading up to the church. Enjoy your pint (and your book).

Studios their

and projects

010 **Accept & Proceed**
www.acceptandproceed.com

HOURS OF DARK (DETAIL) | SCREEN PRINT POSTER | 2008

HOURS OF DARK – WHITE EDITION | SCREEN PRINT POSTER | 2008

How did you start?
Accept and Proceed was founded in 2006 by David Johnston with an ideology to push boundaries and provide inspired and innovative design. Currently, it is in its fourth year of trading, and run by partners David Johnston and Matthew Jones.

What's your background?
David Johnston: Central Saint Martins, Overland, Interbrand, Nike, Red Design. Matthew Jones: Ravensbourne, Spin, The Kitchen, FP7.

Who/what are your main influences? Where/what do you turn to for inspiration?
Muller Brockmann was undoubtedly a revolutionary, so he would be a big influence. But we appreciate all sorts of work and designers, Paul Belford is a master, as is Angus Hyland. We generally love the work of Julian House. We tend not to take influence from current design styles unless the brief requires it.

Do you collect anything? What's on your shelves? And on your walls?
We have a few framed prints on the wall: This year's Light Calendars, Stadttheater June '59, Hacienda 9, and a few of the artists series' from Munich '72.

How would you say the design landscape has changed in, say, the last 10 years?
It's a lot more varied than it was. There are more small companies doing interesting work than there has ever been. I think the rise of the internet and design blogs has been a huge factor for people being able to get their work 'out there' and noticed.

What would you say is the most distinctive characteristic of graphic and the visual arts in the UK?
It's alive, it's interested and engaged.

Where is your studio based, and why?
Bethnal Green. It's the heart of the East End, and our favourite part of London.

011

HOURS OF LIGHT (DETAIL) | SCREEN PRINT POSTER | 2008

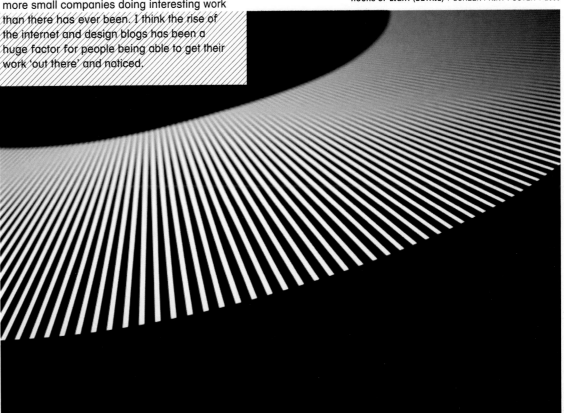

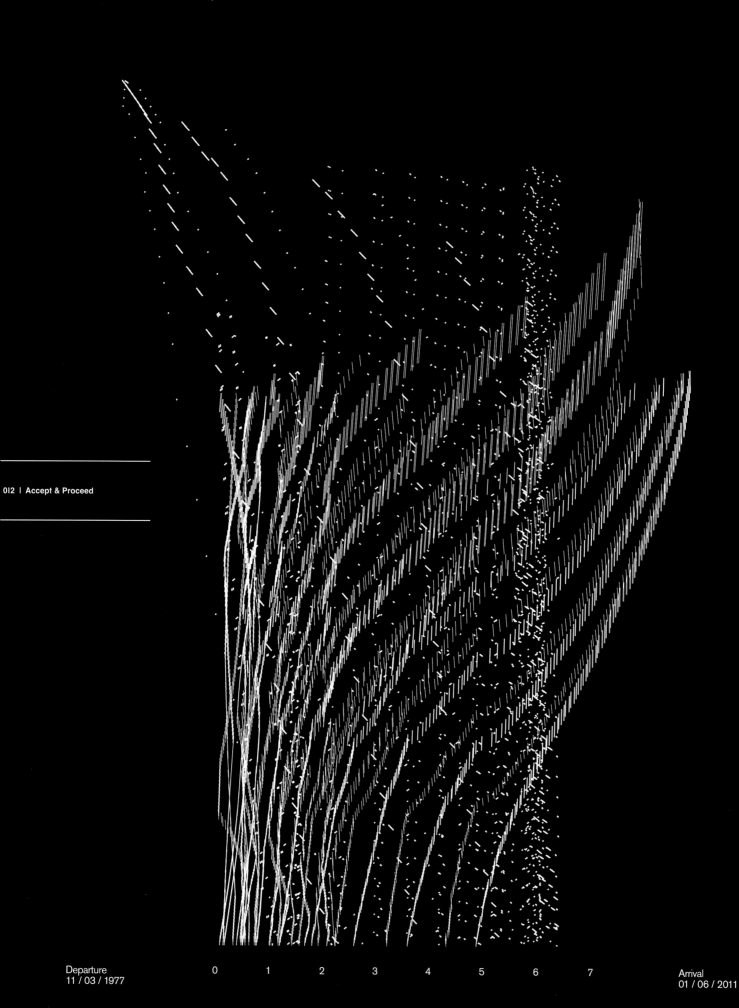

012 | Accept & Proceed

Departure
11 / 03 / 1977

0   1   2   3   4   5   6   7

Arrival
01 / 06 / 2011

OLIGARCH: AQUAVITAE (DETAIL) | CD-SLEEVE

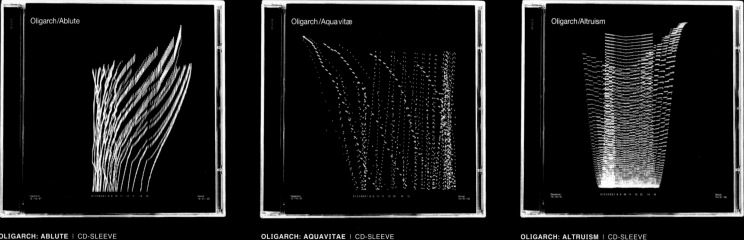

OLIGARCH: ABLUTE | CD-SLEEVE

OLIGARCH: AQUAVITAE | CD-SLEEVE

OLIGARCH: ALTRUISM | CD-SLEEVE

014 | Accept & Proceed

Budapest from the sky

a dog that caught his tail

Hungarian café

the seventy-year old bartender

fat cop

great cover image

What is their background?
Fred studied English at Edinburgh, before moving onto Graphic Design at St Martin's in London, where he also ended up teaching. Nat studied Psychology, including Human Computer Interface at Edinburgh, then moved to London and continued her studies with an MA at the Royal College in Interactive Multimedia. Alex trained and worked in commercial interior design before going on to study Architecture and Interior Design at the Royal College of Art.

Who are your main clients, and what type of work do you mainly do?
It varies wildly, from global companies such as Unilever, Sony and Orange, to non-profit organisations like Greenpeace and individuals – musicians, photographers etc. In the early days, we did a lot of illustration and website projects, as well as being thought of as the "T-shirt People". Clients then started requesting short Flash animations for their websites and, not too long after that, following the dotcom crash, we embarked on several large scale moving image commercial projects having learned the ropes with web animations.

How would you say the design landscape has changed in the last 10 years?
We can only comment from our own point of view. We have consciously moved away from the figurative vector illustration style that established Airside initially. It's great to be known for something, but you have to be allowed to spread your wings (or pencils) and move on. Does that sound like I dodged the question?

How did you start?
Fred and Nat met when they were teenagers at Edinburgh University. They both moved to London and remained in contact. Nat met Alex at the Royal College of Art in London, where they were both doing MAs. Nat introduced Alex to Fred, and shortly after that, when all Mas were finished, and freelance careers had been embarked upon, Airside Studio was born. The idea was that by teaming up with other freelancers and acting like a company, by being in the same large studio, they made clients treat them like a company.

TOP = HYBRIDS | BOTTOM = ALPHABUNNIES
SCREENPRINT FOR AIRSIDE SHOP

What would you say is the most distinctive characteristic of the visual arts in the UK?
Variety. There is no one style like in Japan, where you might pinpoint Manga as a distinctive and outstanding style. Here anything goes as long as someone decides they like it. That's very liberating.

Where is your studio based, and why?
We are based in Islington, London, which is where we've been since the beginning. We only recently moved from our original basement studio in Cross Street to lovely new offices with air and light. Islington is less manic than central London, less expensive than trendy Shoreditch (honestly), and we have tons of cafes, restaurants, shops and grassy knolls to keep us amused at lunchtime.

Where do you live and how do you get to work?
We live in all corners of London and many of us cycle to work. We were very chuffed with the bike storage space we had in the new building, but it's already at capacity and bikes are hanging from the ceiling.

Do you have a favourite place where you often meet up after work?
Lucky Voice karaoke bar just opened up on Upper Street, and we were down there practically on the opening night. Wuthering Heights was sung.

LEFT: MANDALA | SCREENPRINT FOR AIRSIDE SHOP

018 | Airside

FRED DEAKIN'S **TRIPTYCH CD** I LIMITED EDITION BOX I 2008

TOP = FRED DEAKIN'S **TRIPTYCH CD** | LIMITED EDITION BOX
MIDDLE = FRED DEAKIN'S **NU BALEARICA** CD | LIMITED EDITION BOX
BOTTOM = FRED DEAKIN'S **TRIPTYCH** | SAMPLER CD

TRYPTICH | CD-SLEEVE | 2008

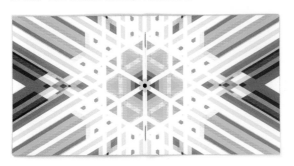

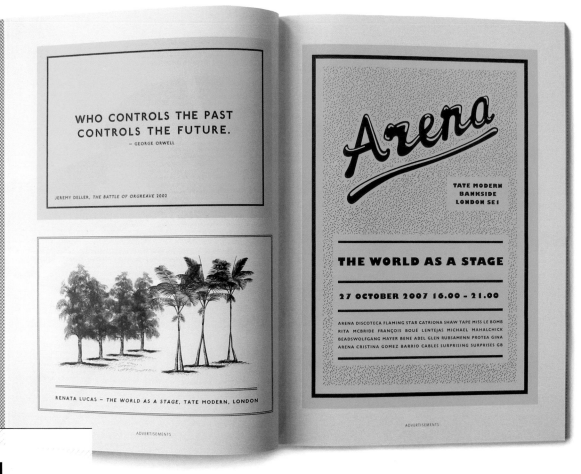

APFEL

www.apracticeforeverydaylife.com

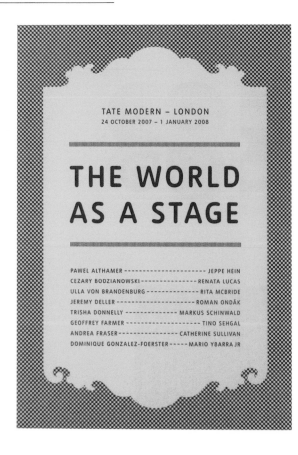

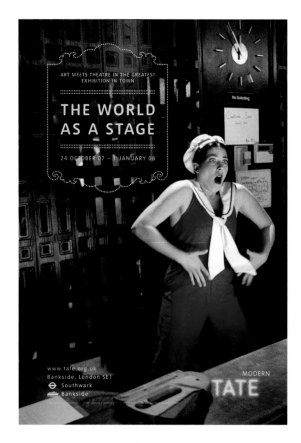

Arena

TATE MODERN
BANKSIDE
LONDON SE1

THE WORLD AS A STAGE

27 OCTOBER 2007 16.00 – 21.00

ARENA DISCOTECA FLAMING STAR CATRIONA SHAW TAPE MISS LE BOMB
RITA MCBRIDE FRANÇOIS BOUÉ LENTEJAS MICHAEL MAHALCHICK
BEADSWOLFGANG MAYER BENE ABEL GLEN RUBSAMENN PROTEA GINA
ARENA CRISTINA GOMEZ BARRIO CABLES SURPRISING SURPRISES GB

MARIO YBARRA JR
**SWEENEY
TATE**
AT TATE MODERN

– The Happy Hypocrite –

LINGUISTIC HARDCORE

for and about experimental art writing

THE HAPPY HYPOCRITE
FOR AND ABOUT EXPERIMENTAL ART WRITING
BIANNUAL JOURNAL
ISSUE I: LINGUISTIC HARDCORE
2008

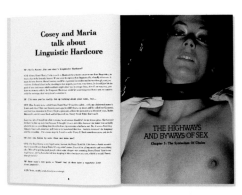

What type of work do you mainly do?

We work predominantly with cultural institutions and individuals i.e. Museums, Galleries, Artists and work with print, editorial, screen, 3-dimensional and promotional material.

How did you start? And why APFEL?

APFEL (A Practice for Everyday Life) was founded by Kirsty Carter and Emma Thomas in 2003. We started working together at the Royal College of Art, and established APFEL on graduating. We were both influenced by a book called *THE PRACTICE OF EVERYDAY LIFE,* by Michel Certeau, in which de Certeau describes his way of making sense of the city with eyes open, collecting materials, drawing together stories – we liked the reference of "practice" as a habit, exercise and pursuit. These practices were the basis of how we wanted to APFEL to work.

Where is your studio based?

Bethnal Green, East London

How many of you are there?

Kirsty and Emma are still the only partners, but we have 2 people full-time with us in the studio and some great help from others along the way.

Do you collect anything? What's on your shelves? And on your walls?

Art works – when working with artists it is great to do an exchange (when you can afford to do this!) It is far more enjoyable to get an artwork at the end of a project than cash; it is the closest we will ever get to collecting. An art work can be a happy reminder of the collaboration for years to come.

How would you say the design landscape has changed in the last 10 years?

We think there has been an increasing awareness of the value of design. The fact that a studio like ours can survive through cultural projects alone is an indication of this; cultural institutions understand they are attracting larger audiences, and design can play a strong role in making this happen. We believe the need for good design will continue to grow and grow.

024

Bark

www.barkdesign.net

What is your background?
Tim Hutchinson studied at St.Martins School of Art & Design for a BA(hons) in graphic design. Jason Edwards studied for his BA(hons) at the University of Brighton. Both studied for a MA in graphic design at the Royal College of Art.

Do you collect anything?
Along with many other design studios our collections underpin a large proportion of our visual database. We were very interested in categorisation a while back. Now we tend to collect in a much looser manner. Each year, we set a collection project to students of the London College Communication, based on the 'Five Hat Rack' principle of categorisation, but make it more intuitive and expressive in terms of how to categorise and analyse a collection.

A MURAL DESIGN FOR A SERIES OF ECLECTIC MUSIC
NIGHTS HELD IN THE CHAMPAGNE BAR OF ANDAZ LIVERPOOL
STREET HOTEL IN LONDON. ACTUAL SIZE — 8 X 13FT | 2009

SIZE: 00.3×0

MAGNUM NITES PRESENTS... MUSIC AT THE CHAMPAGNE BAR

...TURDAYS 7–12PM

How would you say the design landscape has changed in the last 10 years?
The last ten years has seen the advent and growth of the multi-disciplinary design agency, with young professionals not wishing to be pigeon-holed by a single discipline, but to embrace and celebrate the possibilities of being proficient in many skills. The industry has seen a very healthy rise of the small to medium sized design agencies competing successfully against some of the wilting larger companies who ruled over the identity and branding sectors for decades. There's an increasing awareness that small and middle-sized companies can often have greater creative energy within a smaller, more bonded and connected team that can produce equal, if not stronger solutions than the large companies, and at competitive rates.

Who/what are your main influences?
In the early days, the big creatives and artists such as Kurt Schwitters, László Moholy-Nagy, Joseph Albers. Jan Tschichold, Richard Lin, Dan Flavin, and Paul Rand were serious influences and always will be. But more contemporary individuals and groups such as Vaughn Oliver, Graham Wood, 8vo, Pawel Althamer, Alex Seago, Brian Eno, Brian Baderman, Martin Creed and Tim Noble & Sue Webster have all been inspirational in their uniqueness.

What would you say is the most distinctive characteristic of the visual arts in the UK?
An open attitude to possibilities, methodologies, processes and approaches. I see many creative pieces that could only have been conceived and produced in the UK.

025

BEFORE / THIS PLACE

BOOK DESIGN AND ILLUSTRATION FOR TREND PREDICTIONS BOOK *'EMBRACE THE CHAOS'*, AUTHORED BY RICHARD BENSON FOR SHINE COMMUNICATIONS | 2009

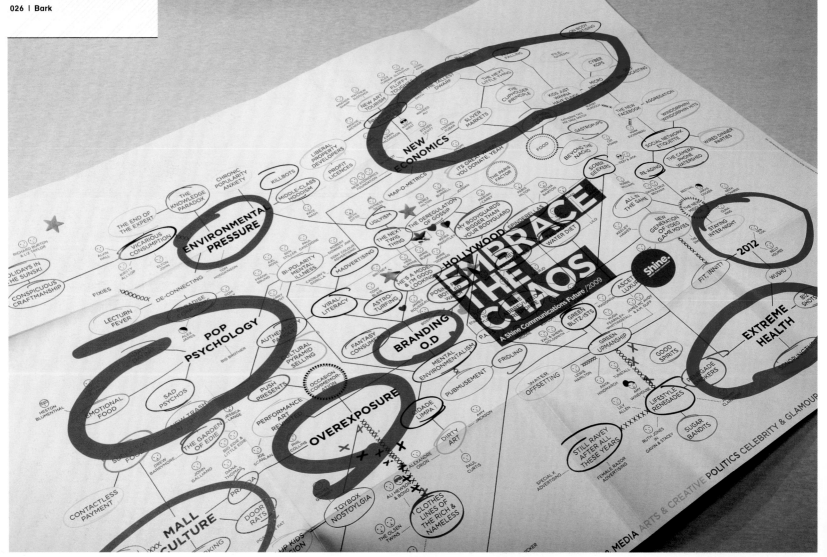

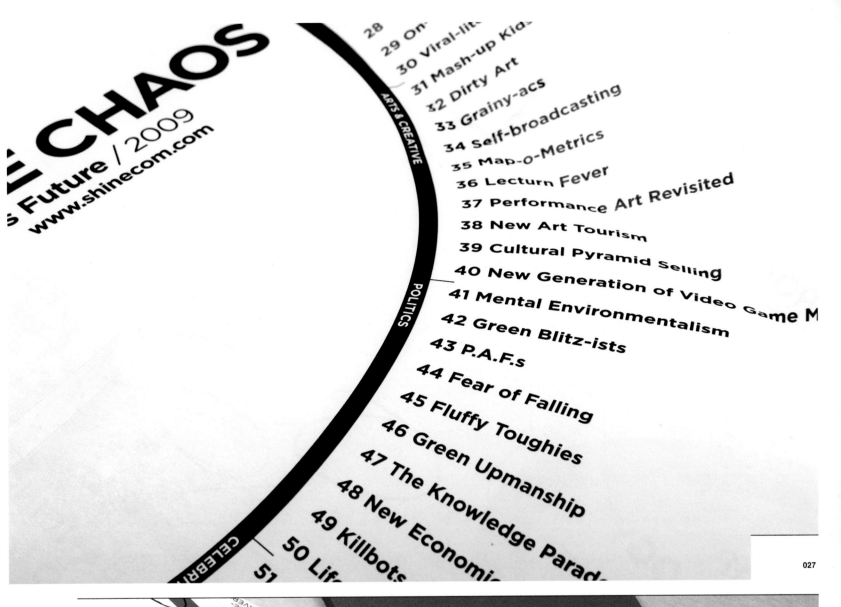

BCMH Bravo Charlie Mike Hotel

www.bcmh.co.uk

Drift
Anne Tallentire

HOUSEY HOUSEY | BOOK
A PATTERN BOOK OF IDEAL HOMES PRESENTS A COLLECTION
OF DESIGN CONCEPTS FOR CONTEMPORARY HOMES

JERWOOD STUDIO AT SADLER'S WELLS
TYPOGRAPHIC IDENTITY SYSTEM

How did you start?
Mark (Hopkins) and I (Ben Chatfield) decided to set up together after we left the RCA. We'd done a few projects together while we were there and then, during the show, we were approached to design two books, one for an architect and one for a small arts publisher, so that's how it started. We had both worked for small design practices before we met at the RCA (Mark had worked at Foundation 33 and I'd worked at Kerr / Noble).

What type of work do you mainly do?
We tend to work for arts-based clients (galleries/institutions/individuals) and architecture practices. Whereas a lot of our work has been for print and exhibition design, we seem to have quite a few identity and branding projects at the moment.

Do you collect anything? What about the others? What's on your shelves? And on your walls?
At the time of writing, we don't have any shelves as we've only just recently moved to our new studio, and so currently all of our books are on the floor (but, obviously, arranged by colour and size).

Who/what are your main influences? Where/what do you turn to for inspiration?
Alan... Annelies... Bruno... Charles... Dieter... Eileen... Enzo... Gerhard... Ian... Jean-Michel... Jimi... Josef... Karel... Keith... Kerri... Larry... Martin... Niklaus... Paul... Pierre... Ray... Yves...

How would you say the design landscape has changed in, say, the last 10 years?
Maybe more human – everything seems a lot more friendly.

029

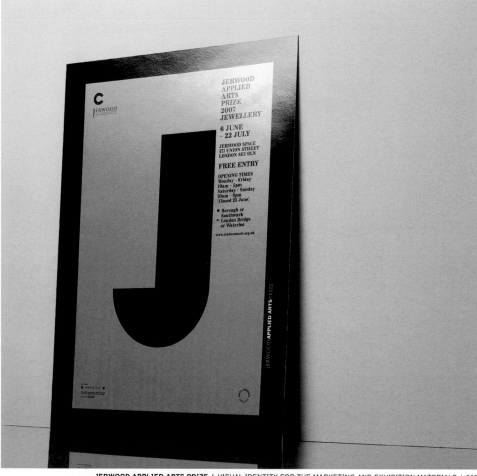

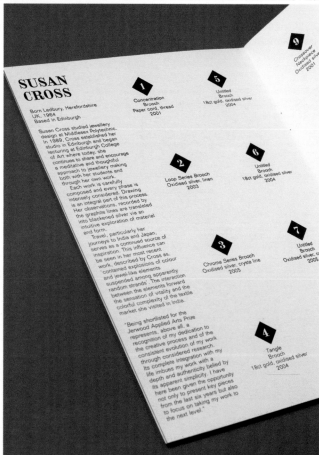

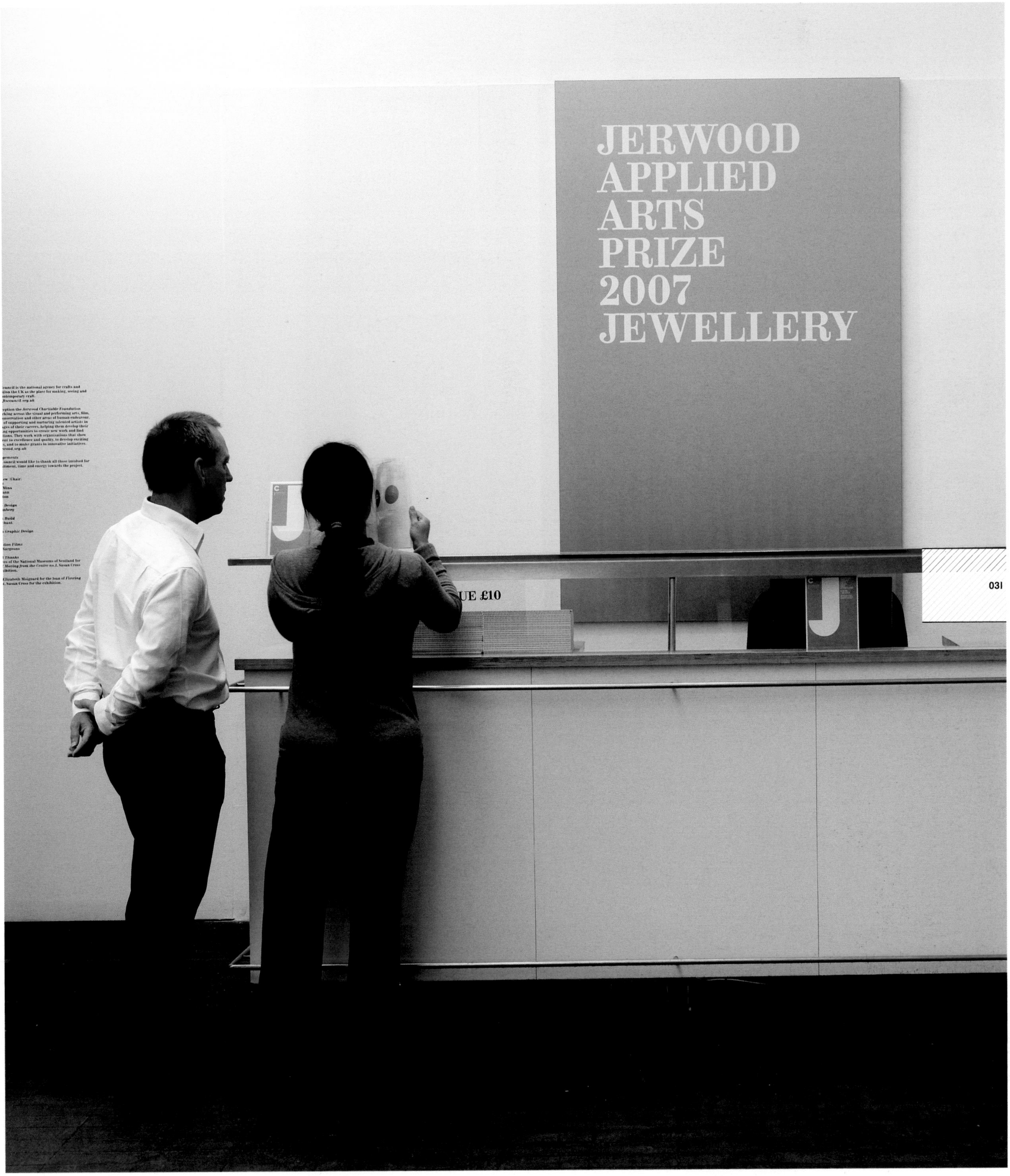
JERWOOD
APPLIED
ARTS
PRIZE
2007
JEWELLERY

Max Braun began by producing components for the fledgling radio industry in Frankfurt. His business grew steadily and began to make its own radio sets. By 1938 Braun employed 1000 people and had introduced the famous logo. Braun prided itself on living up to its responsibilities as an employer. It paid well above the minimum wage and established an innovative and comprehensive health and welfare scheme for all staff.

After Braun's death in 1951, leadership passed to his sons, Artur and Erwin, who began to expand the business into new areas. They looked for new product lines, and developed

After some years of working with outside consultants, including a team from the Ulm school of design (HfG Ulm), Erwin Braun realised that in order to achieve the type of products he visualised, the design leadership would have to come from within Braun.

Rams was quickly promoted within the department, and began to build a young, close-knit team of designers, technicians and model-makers. Under Rams' direction, the design team went on to produce a series of product streams that revolutionised consumer appliances and redefined the image of Braun internationally. Different teams and individuals worked on the various product lines that expanded into television, photography, shaving and kitchen equipment. Within the Braun vocabulary, it is r that there are different gners at work.

res',

eds.

jargon, represent ge

Braun strives to satisfy these needs to the utmost possible extent – even better, perhaps, than the customer could expect.

Braun Brochure

Bibliothèque

www.bibliothequedesign.com

alarm   set   time   world   date   alarm

on   off

BRAUN

How did you start?
We started Bibliothèque around the kitchen table in Jonathon's apartment, this was to be our base of operations for our first six months. Four years on and we have a modest studio in East London. There are five designers in our team – Tim Beard, Jonathon Jeffrey, Sarah Kirby-Ginns, Tom Munckton and Mason Wells. The circumstances behind Bibliothèque were quite organic. The partners had been working for other studios for over a decade. It was the right time to do things for ourselves and gain some independence. The company has three partners – Jonathon, Mason and Tim, but there is minimum hierarchy. Everybody in the studio is a hands-on designer.

What was your background?
Mason and Jonathon met at art school in the late 1980s. Tim and Mason worked together at design studios Cartlidge Levene and North. Jonathon worked at Farrow Design.

What type of work do you mainly do?
We have a wide variety of clients in both the cultural and corporate areas. We like to work in all areas of design. Currently we are working on an identity for the avant-garde music ensemble, The London Sinfonietta and an exhibition at the V&A on the subject of modernism in the cold war period.

Where is your studio based, and why?
It is in the East of London. It is a really creative area that designers of all disciplines seem to gravitate to. Many of our friends are within walking distance so there is a good social aspect.

Do you collect anything? What about the others? What's on your shelves? And on your walls?
Books, posters, design – we are serious about collecting, hence the name Bibliothèque.

Who would you say are your main influences?
We are far more interested in design in the broader sense than just graphic design. Some inspiration: Otl Aicher, Kenya Hara, Jost Hochuli, Rolf Müller, HfG Ulm, Dieter Rams, Super Normal: Naoto Fukasawa / Jasper Morrison, Maarten Van Severen, Poul Kjaerholm, Hans Wegner, Schule für Gestaltung Basel, Nick Roericht.

How would you say the design landscape has changed in the last 10 years?
It is far more fragmented. There are too many magazines and blogs that lack critical analysis.

What would you say is the most distinctive characteristic of graphics in the UK?
There is too much of it.

033

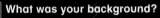
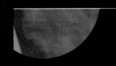
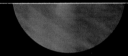
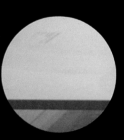

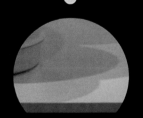

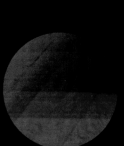
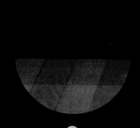
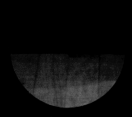
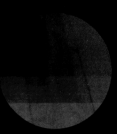
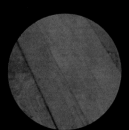

start

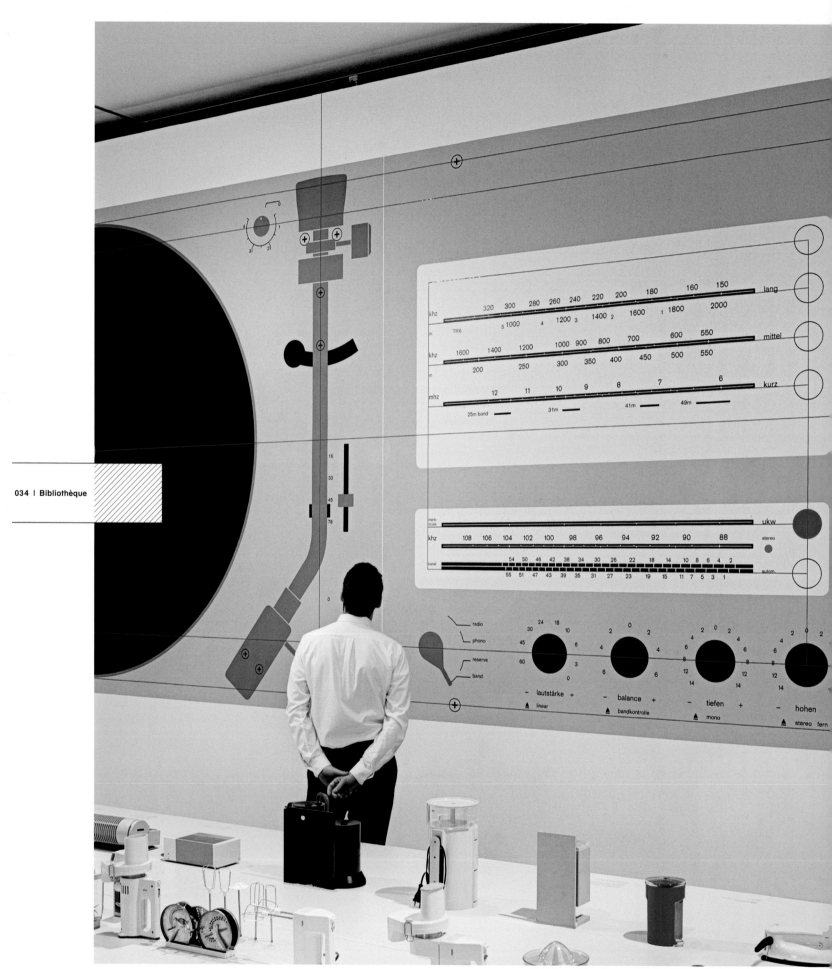

Dieter Rams: ten principles for good design

Based on my experience as a designer, I have distilled the essentials of my design philosophy into ten principles. But these principles cannot be set in stone because, just as technology and culture are constantly developing, so are ideas about good design.

TP 1
radio / phono combination
1959
by Dieter Rams
for Braun

5

Cylindric T 2
lighter
1968
by Dieter Rams
for Braun

6

L 450
flat loudspeaker
TG 60
reel-to-reel tape recorder
TS 45
control unit
1962–64
by Dieter Rams
for Braun

Good design is unobtrusive

Products fulfilling a purpose are like tools. They are neither decorative objects nor works of art. Their design should therefore be both neutral and restrained, to leave room for the user's self-expression.

Good design is honest

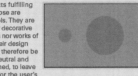

It does not make a product more innovative, powerful or valuable than it really is. It does not attempt to manipulate the consumer with promises that cannot be kept.

1

Good design is innovative

The possibilities for innovation are not, by any means, exhausted. Technological development is always offering new opportunities for innovative design. But innovative design always develops in tandem with innovative technology, and can never be an end in itself.

2

MPZ 21
multipress citrus juicer
1972
by Dieter Rams
and Jürgen Greubel
for Braun

Good design makes a product useful

A product is bought to be used. It has to satisfy certain criteria, not only functional, but also psychological and aesthetic. Good design emphasises the usefulness of a product whilst disregarding anything that could possibly detract from it.

3

Good design is aesthetic

The aesthetic quality of a product is integral to its usefulness because products we use every day affect our person and our well-being. But only well-executed objects can be beautiful.

4

Good design makes a product understandable

It clarifies the product's structure. Better still, it can make the product talk. At best, it is self-explanatory.

T 1000
world receiver
1963
by Dieter Rams
for Braun

8

Good design is thorough down to the last detail

ET 66 calculator
1987
by Dietrich Lubs
for Braun

Nothing must be arbitrary or left to chance. Care and accuracy in the design process show respect towards the consumer.

9

Good design is environmentally-friendly

Design makes an important contribution to the preservation of the environment. It conserves resources and minimises physical and visual pollution throughout the lifecycle of the product.

606 Universal
Shelving System
1960
by Dieter Rams
for Vitsœ

7

Good design is long-lasting

It avoids being fashionable and therefore never appears antiquated. Unlike fashionable design, it lasts many years – even in today's throwaway society.

620 Chair
Programme
1962
by Dieter Rams
for Vitsœ

10

Good design is as little design as possible

Less, but better – because it concentrates on the essential aspects, and the products are not burdened with non-essentials. Back to purity, back to simplicity.

L 2 speaker
1958
by Dieter Rams
for Braun

RT 20 tischsuper radio
1961
by Dieter Rams
for Braun

036 **Browns**

www.brownsdesign.com
www.brownseditions.com
www.jonathanellery.com

How did you start?
Browns was formed in 1998 out of desperation and in response to what was a very corporate and clinical graphic design culture inherent in Britain at that time. The studio is creatively run by founder Jonathan Ellery and Nick Jones, who joined the studio in 2003.

What is their background?
Jonathan Ellery comes from an art background and is originally from Cornwall. Before founding Browns, Ellery worked at design companies including Sampson Tyrell, Addison and Design House, all based in London. Nick Jones prior to Browns worked at Addison, Williams & Phoa and Meta/London.

How would you say the design landscape has changed in the last 10 years?
Massively. British graphic design is now 'generally' made up of two models. Firstly, the large design consultancies that are cash rich, but creatively poor. Secondly, the small design studios that are creatively rich and financially poor. (I'm generalising of course). Both are disappointing for different reasons.

Where is your studio based, and why?
Browns is based in London Bridge, south east London. It inhabits a three storey building, originally a tin can factory built in 1886. The building was purchased by Ellery in 2006 and renovated working with architects Duggan Morris.

Where do you live, how do you get to work?
Jonathan Ellery lives on the third floor of the Browns building and Nick Jones cycles to work from across the river in Clerkenwell.

How many of you work there?
Who gets to pick the music?
Eleven people currently work at Browns made up of designers, two project managers and a financial controller. The music is generally always on. Anyone can pick the music and anyone can turn it off. We've currently been listening to Daft Punk, LCD Sound System, Spiritualised, Juliette & The Licks, The Black Crowes, Ian Brown, the Foofighters and some CD that Alexander Gelman gave us from Tokyo.

Do you collect anything?
Everyone at Browns seem to have developed terrible book habits. Books are very important to us and are very visible in the studio on the shelves.

Do you have a favourite place where you often meet up after work?
The Wheatsheaf public house, Borough Market, SEI.

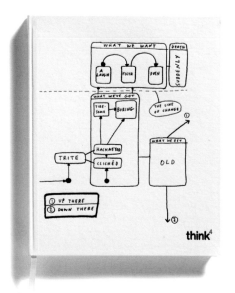

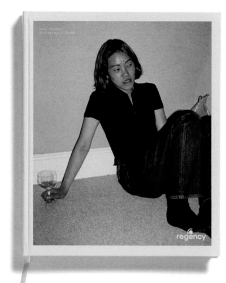

**JOURNALS FOR THE HOWARD SMITH
PAPER LECTURE SERIES.**
GUEST SPEAKERS IN ORDER OF APPEARANCE:
PAUL DAVIS, ALEXANDER GELMAN,
PAUL GRAHAM, LAWRENCE WEINER,
STORM THORGERSON, FELICE VARINI AND
ERIK KESSELS (MAIN IMAGE).
EVENT, DESIGN AND CURATION BY BROWNS.

Invesco

MOTHERS NECKLACE
BOOK IN CONJUNCTION WITH AN
EXHIBITION TO CELEBRATE
THE LAUNCH OF A NEW GLOBAL
IDENTITY FOR INVESCO.
PHOTOGRAPHY BY
DONOVAN WYLIE/MAGNUM.

ELLERY'S THEORY OF NEO-CONSERVATIVE
CREATIONISM. A CATALOGUE
AN EXHIBITION CATALOGUE SHOWING
ARTWORKS THAT HAVE BEEN MACHINED INTO
LARGE SCALE SOLID BRASS PIECES FORMING
PART OF AN ELLERY'S ONE MAN SHOW
AT THE WAPPING PROJECT/LONDON, 2009.
PUBLISHED BY BROWNS EDITIONS.

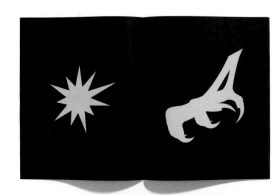

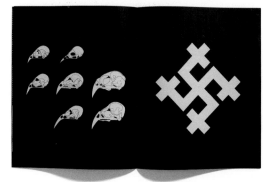

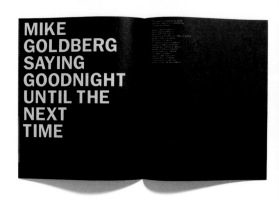

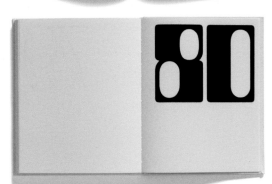

Eighty Seven
Jonathan Ellery ©

First Published July 2006
Ellery/Browns ©

Browns
The Flag Store
29 Queen Elizabeth Street
London SE1 2LP
England
www.brownsdesign.com

All rights reserved. No part of this
publication may be reproduced, stored
in a retrieval system or transmitted,
in any form or by any means, electronic,
mechanical, photocopying, recording
or otherwise without the written
permission of Jonathan Ellery.

87 ELLERY
87 FORMED PART OF ELLERY'S FIRST MAJOR SHOW
AT THE WAPPING PROJECT IN LONDON, 2006.
SHOWN AS A LARGE SCALE INSTALLATION WITH SOUND
AND MOVING IMAGE, ELLERY LOOKS AT NUMBERS
OUT OF CONTEXT, ENABLING THEM TO BE SEEN IN THE
ABSTRACT. PUBLISHED BY BROWNS EDITIONS.

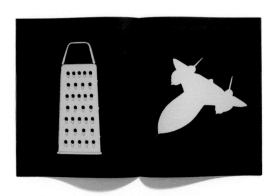
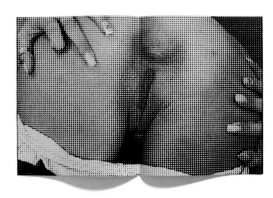

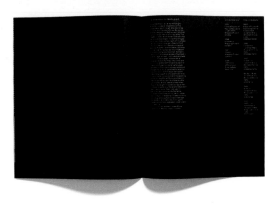

DEATH

Triptych-1
wearebuild.com
3of3

Build
www.wearebuild.com

DEATH | +8I/THE NORTH FACE | PART THREE
OF A TRIPTYCH FOR THE NORTH FACE, JAPAN | 2008

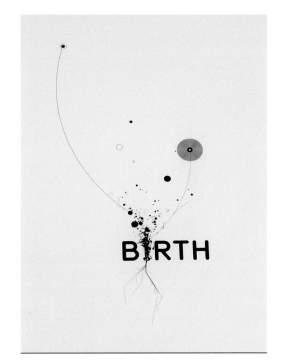

How did you start?
With a lot of hard work. Build is Michael (Place) & Nicky [& currently Guy who is free-lancing with us]. We set up the studio as we wanted to be able to do the things we wanted to do for the people we want to work with. We both quit our jobs in good companies, then travelled the world for a year, then set up the company.I (Michael) studied in Newcastle, then worked at Bite It! with Trevor Jackson, then at TDR in Sheffield for 10 years. Nicky studied Illustration at college, then went into video games as a game artist (in the days of 2D pixel artwork!). A few years later the company she worked for (Psygnosis) was working on Wipeout, a launch title for the first Playstation. Nicky was the Lead Artist on the project and TDR was commissioned to work on it – and that's how we met.

Where is your studio based, and why?
Walthamstow, E17 (North East London), on the end of the Victoria line. Why? Because it's close to home, and it's great to be off the beaten track. We like to think it shows a sense of confidence in what we do.

BIRTH | +81/THE NORTH FACE | PART ONE
OF A TRIPTYCH FOR THE NORTH FACE, JAPAN | 2008

Where do you live, how do you get to work?
Walthamstow, E17. Out the door, turn left, continue forward, over the road, at the top of the road turn left, then right, over the road, up the mews, right through the door, up the stairs, through the door, right again, through the door, approximately 9 minutes total journey time.

Do you have a favourite place where you often meet up after work?
B: There's a few places we go. One is a nice pub in an area of Walthamstow called 'The Village' called the Nags Head, it has a lovely beer garden (weather permitting) and we often go up there to relax and discuss work [or with a friend last night, the wonders of Freehand!].

Do you collect anything?
I collect Letraset catalogues (sad, I know). Nicky doesn't, well not for the studio anyway. We have a variety of books, paper samples, 5 MeBoxes, 2 large King Kens, I small King Ken (in wrestling gear), CDs, tin robot, magazines, New York subway guide (1972), Build embossing tool, ARENA X-Award, Hair Portrait card by Mr Bingo & some DVDs. We have a couple of framed prints propped against the wall & an engraved frame from our On/Off show. We also have number of boxes of things that are just nice (sweet wrappers, postcards, biscuits in smiley wrappers etc.)

How would you say the design landscape has changed in the last 10 years?
I think it's faster, it's the age of 'broadband thinking', things move along at a much quicker pace, things are discarded very quickly. People are losing a bit of craft.

What would you say is the most distinctive characteristic of the visual arts in the UK?
Sense of style, sense of humour.

THOUGHT | +81/THE NORTH FACE | EXHIBITION POSTER
FOR THE NORTH FACE, JAPAN | 2008

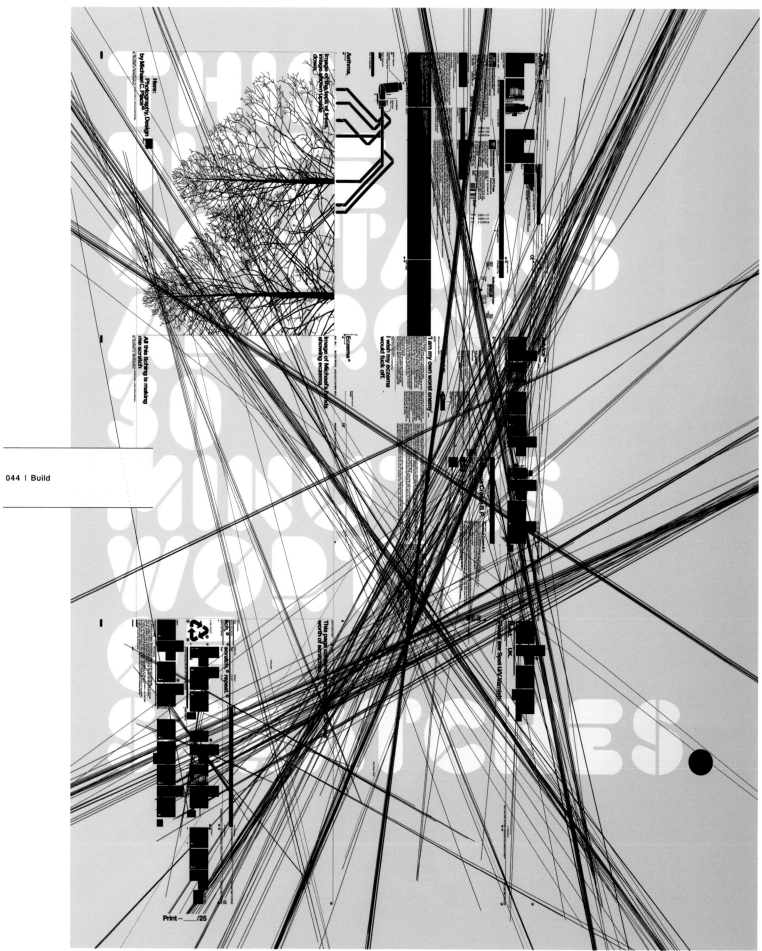

044 | Build

SCRATCH | MAXALOT | POSTER DESIGN FOR THE BUILD/COMMONWEALTH SHOW 'ON/OFF', BROOKLYN/NEW YORK, USA. | 2006

TOP ROW: MOODSTREAM™ | GETTY IMAGES | PROMOTIONAL POSTCARD SET FOR THE GETTY IMAGES SEARCH TOOL 'MOODSTREAM' | 2008

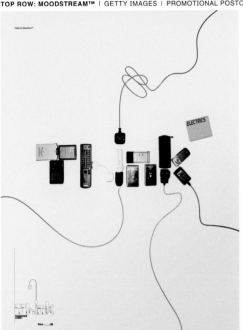

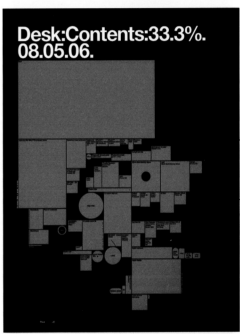

MIDDLE ROW: THINK IN ELECTRICS - TAKEO - MY DESK ON MONDAY | MAXALOT | VARIOUS POSTER DESIGNS FOR THE BUILD/COMMONWEALTH SHOW 'ON/OFF', BROOKLYN/NEW YORK, USA. | 2006

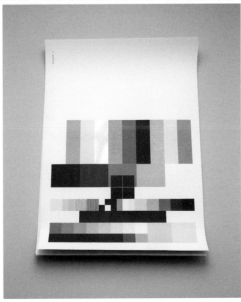

BOTTOM ROW: NOT FOR COMMERCIAL USE/PASTE | GENERATION PRESS/BUILD | ONGOING SERIES OF COLLABORATIVE WORK BETWEEN GENERATION PRESS & BUILD | 2006

Peace

and Love, Build.

PEACE AND LOVE
BUILD | SELF PROMOTIONAL POSTER | 2003

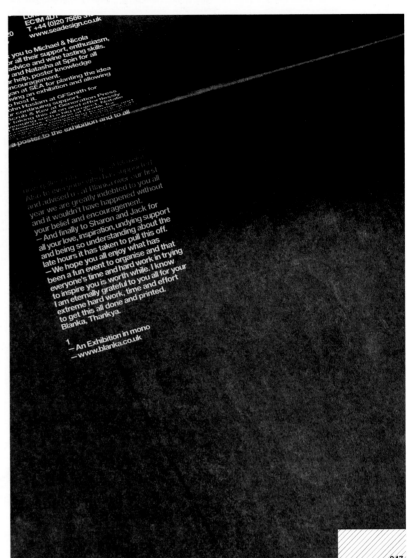

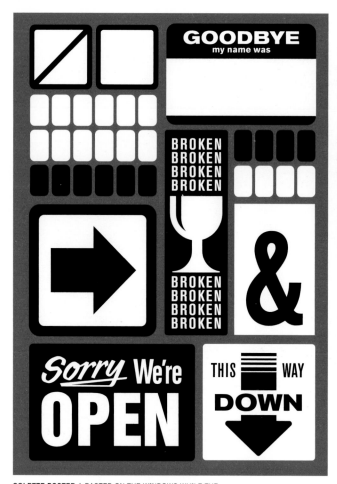

COLETTE POSTER | PASTED ON THE WINDOWS WHILE THE
PARISIAN SHOP WAS CLOSED FOR RENOVATION

Anthony Burrill

www.anthonyburrill.com

LIBERTY CAR WASH | PRESS AND POSTER CAMPAIGN FOR A
LOCAL CAR WASH IN UTRECHT, THE NETHERLANDS

WELCOME TO LONDON

LEFT: IMAGE FOR PRINT SERIES
'IF YOU COULD DO ANYTHING TOMORROW –
WHAT WOULD IT BE?',
PUBLISHED BY IFYOUCOULD

How did you start?

I studied graphic design at the Royal College of Art in the early nineties. That experience made me think I could set up my own studio and work independently. So that's what I did. For the first few years I worked on the dining room table in my girlfriend's house in South London. Making everything without the aid of a computer. I hand set photocopied type and drew simple illustrations. That's when I developed my aesthetic, more by accident than design. I've always been fiercely independent. I've never worked in a design studio. Perhaps that's why it took me so long to work out what I wanted to do.

Where are you from?

I am originally from the North of England and I grew up in a semi-industrial / rural area. I've got a fully developed Northern sense of humour. I use it all the time. My upbringing is engrained in my work.

Who do you do work for?

My main clients are in advertising. I've work-ed on a number of high profile campaigns, DIESEL, Bupa, The Economist, Hans Brinker Budget Hotel. I have agents in London and New York who market my work to advertising companies. I also gener-ate a lot of side projects. I have worked with musicians, architects, and writers and smaller projects.

Where's your studio based?

My studio is built next to my house in a small village in the heart of rural Kent. The setting is extremely tranquil. My work and home life overlap a great deal. My wife and I have two children, so it is nice to work at home and see the children when they come home from school. I'm normally in the studio at 9.00 in the morning. I work till the children get home from school at 3.30. Then usually pop back to the studio for a couple of hours in the evening.

Do you collect stuff?

I try not to collect too many things. I like books and have got an extensive reference library. I try to produce more than I consume. The studio is very tidy. I'm quite obsessive about all that. I can't stand clutter and get rid of any-thing that I haven't used recently.

What would you say were your influences?

I can't really identify specific influences. I have always loved the work of Eduardo Paolozzi, I get a lot of inspiration from his work and from his life as an artist.

How did the design world change in the last 10 years?

Hugely, the internet has changed everything. Now communication is so easy, and we have so many opportunities to reach out to like minded people. It's almost overwhelming the amount of information that is freely available. I think the key is to know how to edit all the information, so you can use it wisely.

What would, you say, characterises design in the UK?

Individuality.

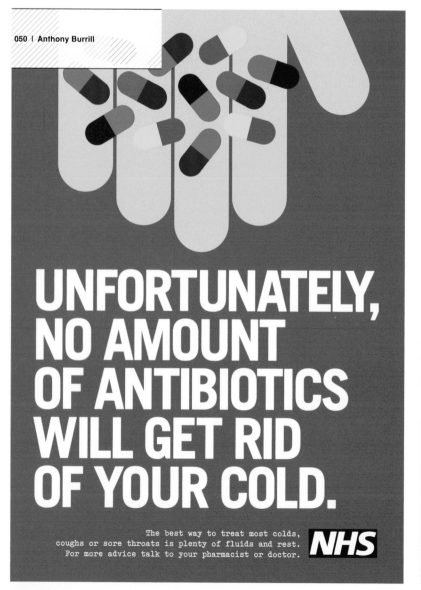

UNFORTUNATELY, NO AMOUNT OF ANTIBIOTICS WILL GET RID OF YOUR COLD.

The best way to treat most colds, coughs or sore throats is plenty of fluids and rest. For more advice talk to your pharmacist or doctor. **NHS**

REMEMBER, ANTIBIOTICS WON'T HELP YOUR DEFENCES AGAINST A COLD.

The best way to treat most colds, coughs or sore throats is plenty of fluids and rest. For more advice talk to your pharmacist or doctor. **NHS**

I LIKE
IT, WHAT
IS IT?

NO
THANK
YOU.

BARBICAN ARTS CENTER | SIGNAGE SYSTEM | 2007

Cartlidge Levene

www.cartlidgelevene.co.uk

How did you start?
Cartlidge Levene was started in 1987 by
Ian Cartlidge and Adam Levene. After working
for large multi-disciplined design consultancies, we decided that smaller, personal,
inti-mate and creative was better.

What was your background?
Conran Design Group, Michael Peters
Literature. Met at 'Design Solution' in 1985.

Who are your main clients?
Currently, Selfridges, V&A, Tate Modern,
Guardian News & Media, Phaidon Press,
Stanton Williams Architects, SMC Alsop. Work
ranges from Wayfinding and Environmen-
tal Graphics, Identity, Print and Digital media.

Where is your studio based?
St John Street in Clerkenwell, London.
It's near to where some of us live and a great area to live and work.

Do you have a favourite place where you often meet up after work?
The Peasant, St John Street

How would you describe your studio?
Clean, cluttered and carefully thought out all rolled into one. Our favourite feature is a huge pinboard covering one wall where all work gets pinned up, discussed, argued over, tweaked and adjusted.

What are your main influences?
All good, intelligent, original graphic design, architecture, art and writing.
Also the everyday and the ordinary.

CARSTEN HÖLLER'S 'TEST SITE' CATALOGUE
THE SEVENTH UNILEVER SERIES INSTALLATION AT
THE TURBINE HALL AT TATE MODERN.

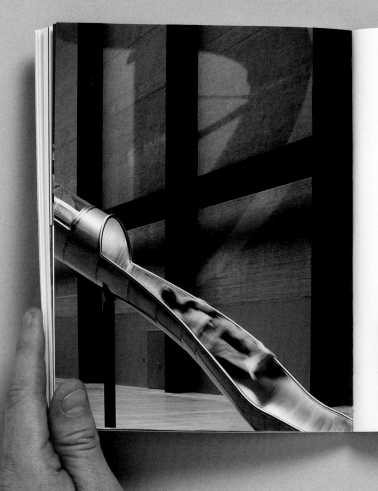

Elevations
Bibliography
Credits

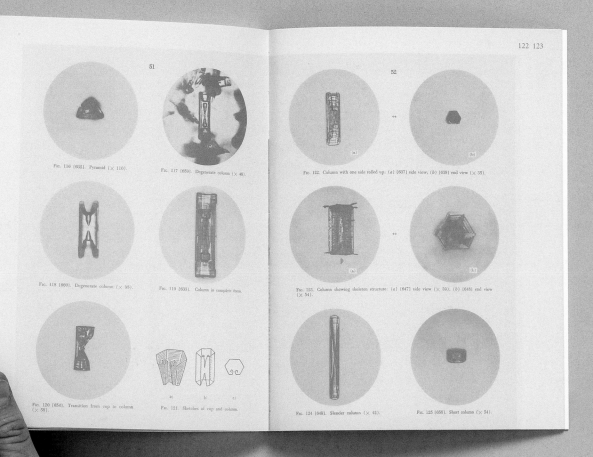

51

FIG. 116 [655]. Pyramid (× 110).

FIG. 117 [659]. Degenerate column (× 48).

FIG. 118 [660]. Degenerate column (× 95).

FIG. 119 [635]. Column in complete form.

FIG. 120 [654]. Transition from cup to column (× 58).

FIG. 121. Sketches of cup and column.

a)   b)   c)

52

FIG. 122. Column with one side rolled up: (a) [637] side view, (b) [658] end view (× 55).

FIG. 123. Column showing skeleton structure: (a) [647] side view, (× 59), (b) [645] end view (× 54).

FIG. 124 [649]. Slender column (× 42).

FIG. 125 [656]. Short column (× 54).

Matt Dent

www.mattdent.com

NEW UK COIN DESIGNS

THE IMAGE SPREADING OVER THE 6 COINS TOOK
HERALDIC FORM IN THE SHAPE OF THE SHIELD
OF THE ROYAL ARMS. THE POUND COIN WAS ADDED TO
THE SET TO DEPICT, DEFINE AND SUPPORT THE
ENTIRE DESIGN. THE IDEA WAS CHOSEN BY THE ROYAL
MINT'S ADVISORY COMMITTEE AND APPROVED BY
THE CHANCELLOR (THEN MR BROWN) AND THE QUEEN

MATT DENT: "COINS THAT ACT AS JIGSAW PIECES.
AN UNPRECEDENTED APPROACH TO COINAGE THAT
HAS GOT PEOPLE OF ALL AGES LOOKING AT THE COINS
IN THEIR HANDS IN A NEW LIGHT."

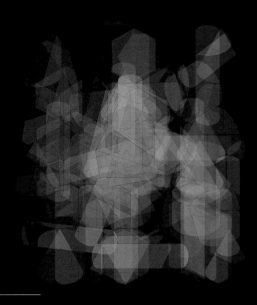

How did you start?
My first recollection of really enjoying art and design was when I was suffering with glandular fever at about 8 years old and found a dinosaur book to copy. I grew up in north Wales, only leaving to focus on graphic design at Brighton, then migrated to London, which I'm loving. In the daytime I'm working with the IO person strong design agency 3 fish in a tree. Beyond the studio I try and do my own thing. I think it's important to stretch yourself beyond the confines of paid work and real clients, and sometimes you just need to stay in touch with the reasons you do what you do.

What kind of work do you mostly do?
I get my kicks from trying a real mixture of work: print – yes, web – yes, photography – yes, 3D – why not. I'm attracted by things that have a bit of humour, and am interested in things which are initially beyond my understanding and comfort zone, the coin designs are a good example of this.

Where do you work from?
Beyond 3 fish I'm working at home in south west London. Because it's a small flat the studio blurs with the lounge, the right angles of the studio bits meet the comfy angles of the lounge stuff. It's not ideal, but at least I'm in touch with what my girlfriend is watching in *Neighbours*.

What's on your walls, on your shelves?
The Experimental Jetset poster for the Helvetica film is propped up against the wall next to a painting by John Elwyn. Photography books sit cover to cover with science books, illustration books face the Harry Potter series. The studio meets the lounge.

059

How do you see graphics in the UK today?
Borders are blurring: graphic design is progressively more involved with other disciplines. It's a great thing.

DESIGN TRENDS
ARE THERE TRENDS IN DESIGN BETWEEN
DIFFERENT PROFESSIONS?
20 COUNTY PLANNERS, 20 BUILDERS, 20 GRAPHIC
DESIGNERS AND 20 ILLUSTRATORS WERE
GIVEN 6 DIFFERENT SHAPES OF 6 DIFFERENT
COLOURS. WOULD ONE AVERAGE GROUP DESIGN
DIFFER SIGNIFICANTLY FROM THE NEXT?

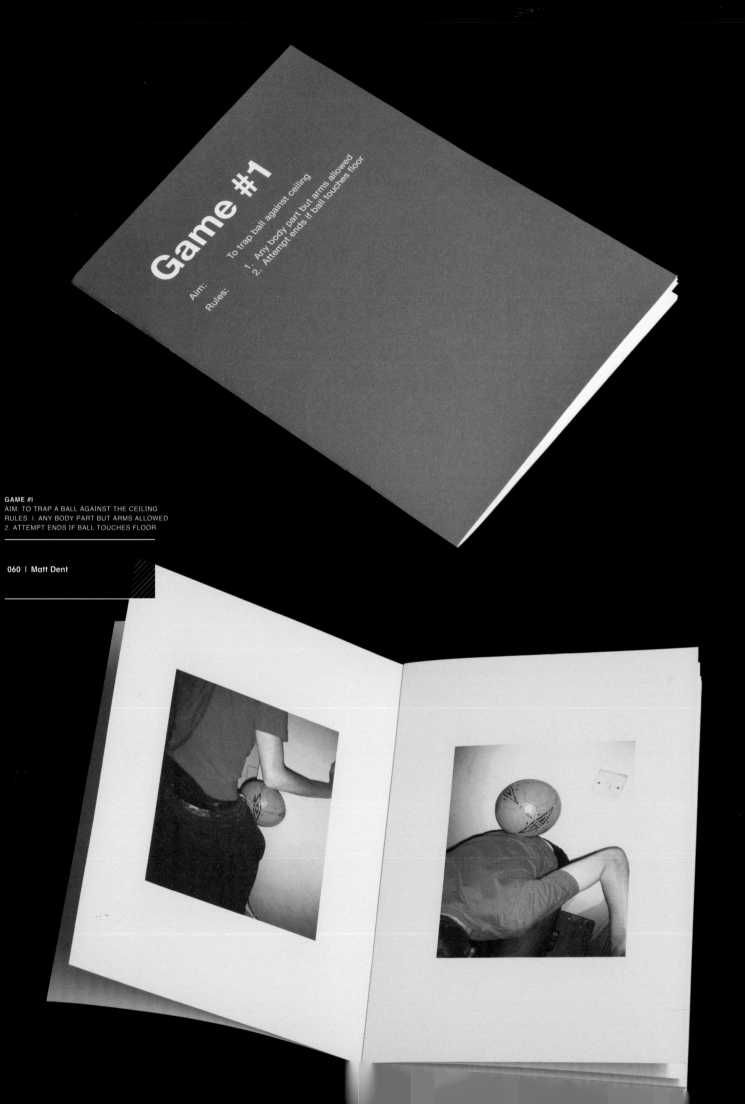

GAME #I
AIM: TO TRAP A BALL AGAINST THE CEILING
RULES: I. ANY BODY PART BUT ARMS ALLOWED
2. ATTEMPT ENDS IF BALL TOUCHES FLOOR

060 | Matt Dent

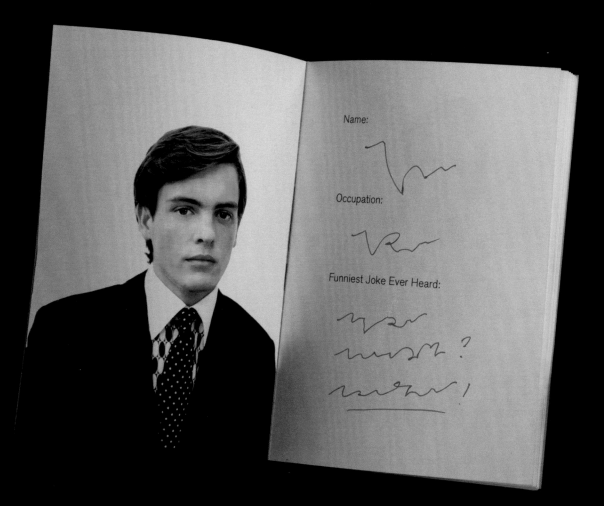

Name:

Occupation:

Funniest Joke Ever Heard:

BRITAIN'S 10 MOST ILLEGIBLE BACHELORS
A SPIN ON THE ALL TOO POPULAR ELIGIBLE
BACHELOR COMPILATIONS OF TRASHY
GIRLY MAGAZINES. FEATURES 10 DISADVAN-
TAGED MALES.

BRITAIN'S 10 MOST
ILLEGIBLE BACHELORS

Unusual printing surfaces
Experimenting with paper, board
and plastic substrates

This 64 page specimen
booklet utilises 16
unusual printing
surfaces taken from
the Curious Collection.

The Curious Collection
is a unique laboratory
developed range
of papers, boards
and plastics—all with
enhanced aesthetic
surface properties.
The collection is made
of five ranges:
Translucents, Particles,
Metallics, Touch and

Particles are recycled
sheets with variations
of pronounced fibres,
all with differing
characteristics.
Some grades have
thermochromic
qualities (altering
in colour after a
temperature change)
while others shimmer
in the light or have
colour coordinated
flecks that add a unique
dimension to the
surface.

[...]
of
[...] for the
[...] to provide
[...]ss point to the
[...]es and encourage
further investigation
of the collection.

Range includes 12
colours, 3 weights
(100–250g),
2 envelopes (C5 and DL)

Page 19.20 45.46
Hot Ice 100g

Translucents   Particles   Metallics   Tou

062

Design Project

www.designproject.co.uk

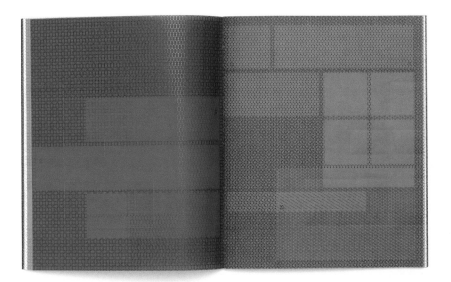

How did you start?

We had both have been in the industry working as graphic designers for over 17 years, and we felt that the only way to create the kind of work we wanted to produce was to have as much control over what we were doing as possible. No account handlers, print buyers, marketing execs – just designers. The best designers, in our opinion, have the inbuilt ability to question everything about the jobs they produce and in a lot of ways are a number of people rolled into one. Running a design business heightens this by way of you having to wear a multitude of hats at any time. It's this ability that we think ultimately gives a good designer more power. By understanding absolutely everything about the jobs you work on whether it be the budget, the market or the production processes you have at your disposal, it is only then that you can decide on the most appropriate solution.

What type of work do you mainly do?

We have mainly been concentrating on cultural projects for artists and arts organizations, but have also done a number of things with businesses who need to target the creative industry. Our way of working seems to produce work that designers find appealing. I think it must be the combination of detail and flair.

TOP AND BELOW: ARJO WIGGINS FINE PAPERS
PRODUCT BROCHURE, INSIDE DETAILS

Where is your studio based, and why?

Our studio is based in the centre of Leeds. It's a centre for design in the north and has all the support services close to hand that we require.

How would you say the design landscape has changed in the last 10 years?

Things have changed quite a lot. Over the last few years we have seen a return to craft, which is obviously the flip side of the technology revolution.

What would you say is the most distinctive characteristic of the visual arts in the UK?

The best UK work is visually economic, crafted, ordered, articulate and memorable.

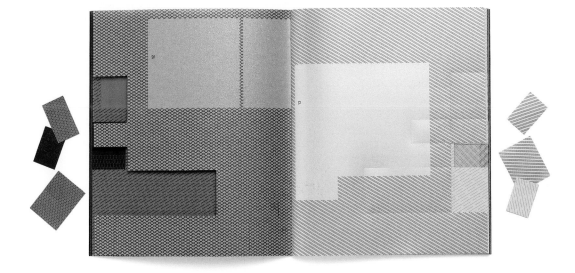

Hello Friends
by Bryan and Laura Davies

HELLO FRIENDS | MONOGRAPH, ON-SCREEN BRANDING
AND CONTENT MAN AGED WEBSITE FOR BRYAN AND
LAURA DAVIES, ARTISTS SPECIALISING IN SCULPTURE AND
SMALL ARCHITECTURAL STRUCTURES.

Studio

__ Working out the sculpture's
vertical narrative with books
on the studio floor
__ Maquette with developing
image narrative
__ Model in progress for the
ceremonial structure image

Development

__ The apparatus used to cast
shadows for the cave painting
image
__ Test shot of the unfinished
space station model
__ Setting up the city square model
to be photographed
__ Testing a fibreglass rhomboid
module at Design and Display
Structures, London

Installation

__ The structural steel of the
sculpture at Bridgewater Place
atrium
__ View of the open illuminated
light boxes
__ Lowering the final rhomboid
into position
__ Installation scaffold in the
atrium

Hello Friends
by Bryan and Laura Davies

PROGRESS PACKAGING
IDENTITY AND BRAND APPLICATION

Work in packaging

Progress Packaging

Progress are a unique market leading company. Production knows and understands most production formats, whilst able to manage production.

Our aim is to whilst move production. Our client best to manage Progress Packaging. We are able to Working able to Progress Packaging.

specialising in the we provide exptertise, a profession from concept to an end result. The production knows how to any innovating as immediate, as our clients when make concept most formats.

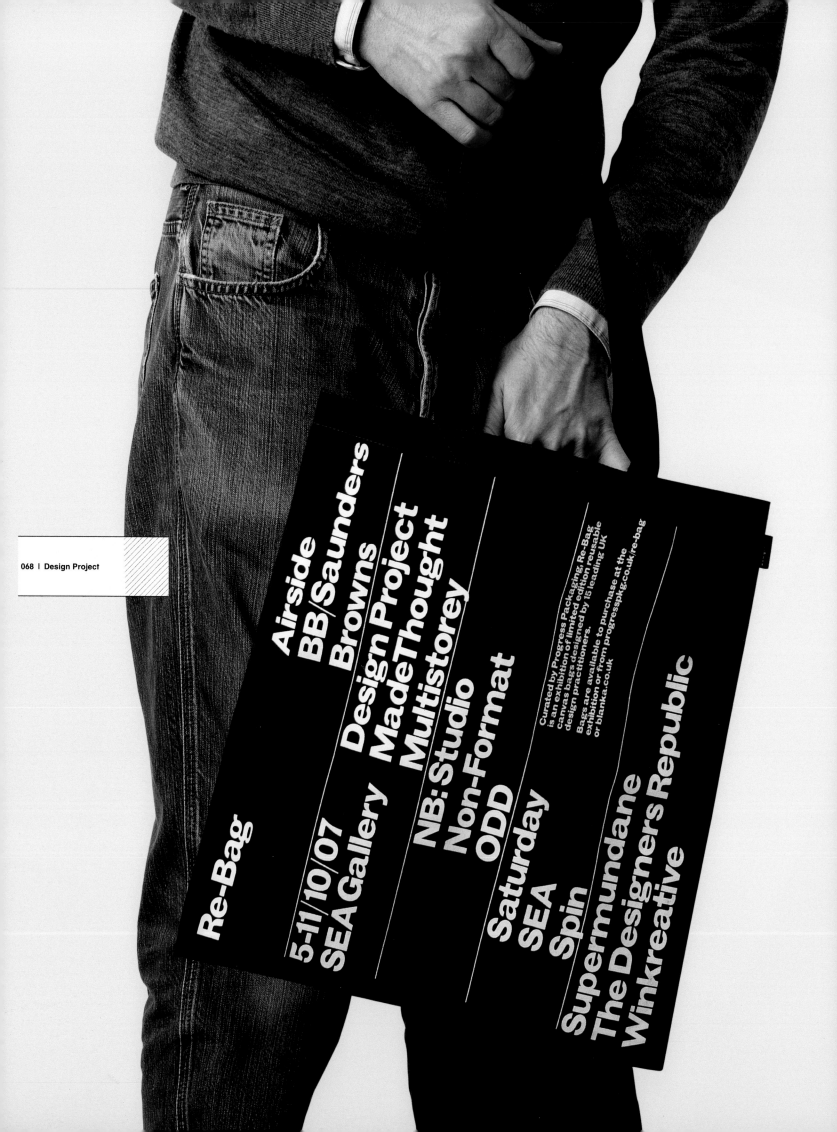

Re-Bag

5-11/10/07
SEA Gallery

Airside
BB/Saunders
Browns
Design Project
MadeThought
Multistorey
NB: Studio
Non-Format
ODD
Saturday
SEA
Spin
Supermundane
The Designers Republic
Winkreative

Curated by Progress Packaging, Re-Bag
is an exhibition of limited edition
canvas bags designed by 15 leading UK
design practitioners.
Bags are available to purchase at the
exhibition or from progresspkg.co.uk/re-bag
or blanka.co.uk

PROGRESS PACKAGING: RE-BAG | PROMOTIONAL BAG (LEFT PAGE) CARDS AND POSTER | 2007

Design Project /1
the Typographic
Circle /2
8. May 2007 /3

Team Impression /4
GF Smith /5

1 Design Project (formed
  in 2004 by Andy Probert
  and James Littlewood)
  are a graphic design
  consultancy that work
  for a variety of business
  and cultural organisations
  across the UK. In 2006
  D&AD commissioned
  Design Project to design
  their highly prestigious
  44th Annual of the best
  in international design,
  advertising and creative
  communication.

2 Formed in 1976, the
  Typographic Circle are a
  not-for-profit organisation
  run entirely by volunteers.
  Through lectures, exhibitions
  and debates it brings
  together anyone with
  an active interest in type
  and typography.

3 Venue:
  LCB Depot — Leicester.

4 Print sponsorship:
  Team Impression (Offset
  litho overprinted 2 colours
  with foil block).

5 Paper sponsorship:
  GF Smith (PhoeniXmotion
  150gsm).

Poster by Design Project
Leeds and Manchester

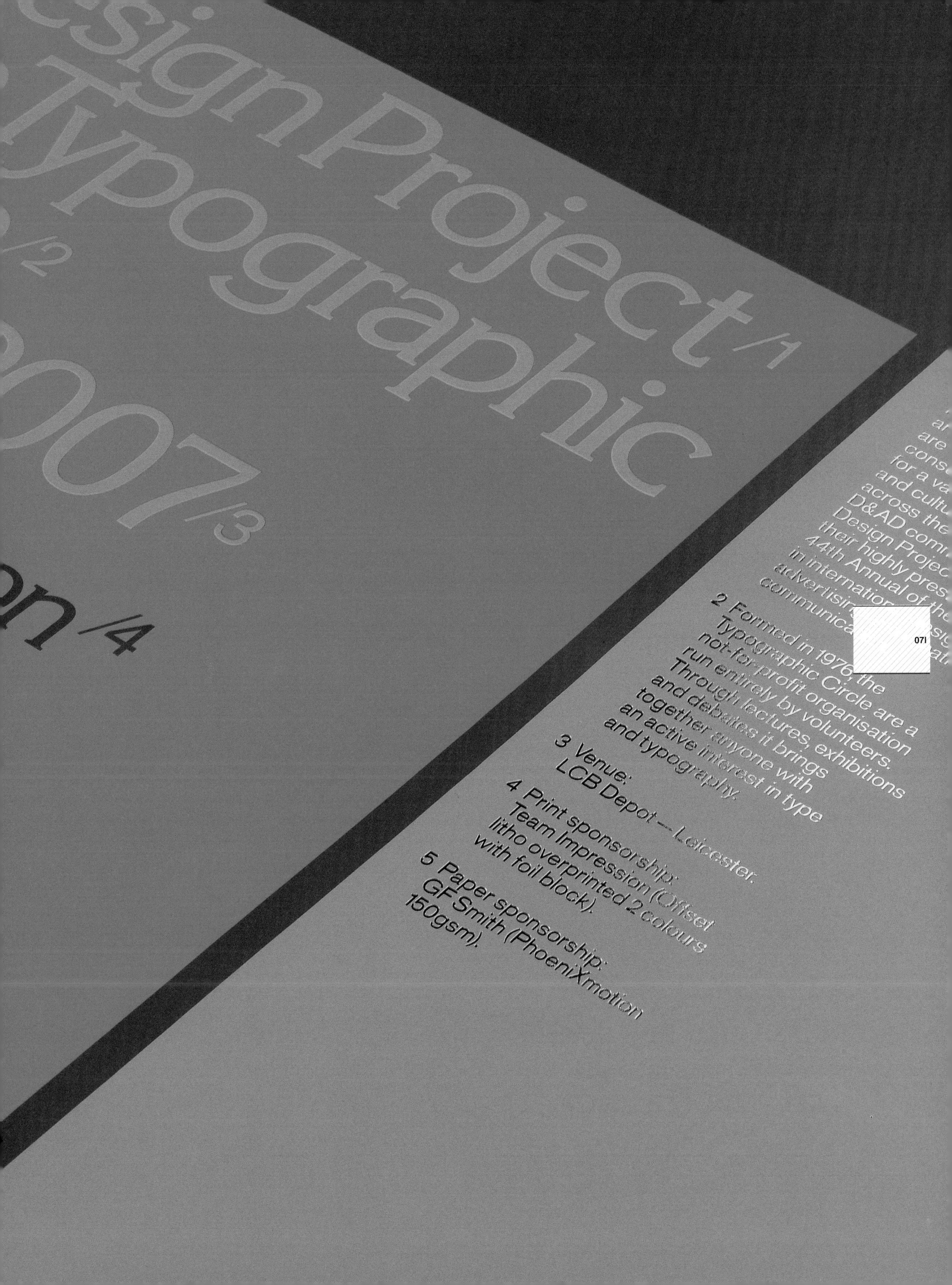

Design Project /1

Typographic /2

2007 /3

...on /4

...ar...
...are
...consu...
for a va...
and cultu...
across the...
D&AD com...
Design Projec...
their highly pres...
44th Annual of th...
in internationa...
advertising...
communica...

2 Formed in 1976, the Typographic Circle are a not-for-profit organisation run entirely by volunteers. Through lectures, exhibitions and debates it brings together anyone with an active interest in type and typography.

3 Venue: LCB Depot — Leicester.

4 Print sponsorship: Team Impression (Offset litho overprinted 2 colours with foil block).

5 Paper sponsorship: GF Smith (PhoeniXmotion 150gsm).

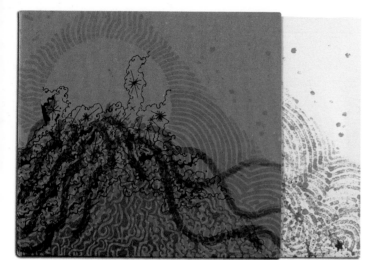

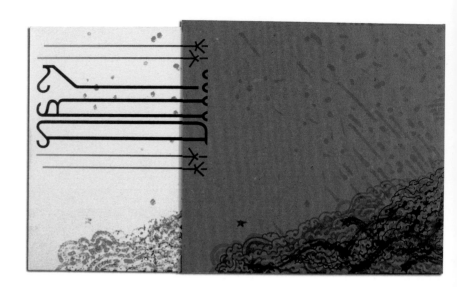

TOP LINE: DR WHO DAT? | CD PACKAGING & LP INNERSLEEVES | 2005

ehquestionmark

www.ehquestionmark.com

How did you start?

We met through misanthropy. Our clique published Hold No Hostage, a UK graffiti magazine and our roster of typographically gifted friends grew exponentially, so ehquestionmark was founded as a way to work as a collaborative. We're a UK based artists collab comprised of members bound by a passion for typography, although each having their own time-served disciplines, projects and fields of expertise. We specialise in the mediums of print, painting and sculpture. Other communicative mediums are also employed, such as haute couture, screen / time-based and installation art.

Who are your main clients, and what type of work do you mainly do?

Lex Records, Skam Recordings, Pollinaria – they are our main clients, but we work on many other projects and consider anything. It's all about the challenge, adventure and the faith of the commissioner. Most of our work is art led as opposed to design led, design is our funding for our own projects.

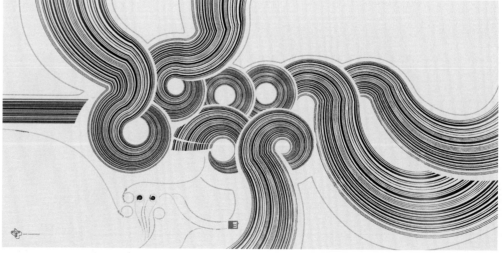

BOOM BIP | LP RECORD SLEEVE – FRONT & BACK | 2002

What time do you usually get to work?
What time do you leave?
Masochistically and ambitiously open 24-7.
We are secular ascetic martyrs that use sleep
deprivation as a cheap intoxicant.

How would you describe your studio?
Random organised chaos - with a bed in the
vicinity.

Do you collect anything?
We're hoarders of objet-trouvé, disposable
ephemera and worthless bric-a-brac tat - eg.
A collection of discarded vintage
drinks cans excavated from rail-side land.

What are your main influences?
Everything, anything, everyday, any day,
unprescribable and unexpectably random.
A walk in a rat infested, dense cosmopolitan city will suffice when times are dry
and inspiration is needed, although a
walk anywhere is full of surprises - simply
letting neuro-aesthetics do the work.
Carboot sales are a great form of contemporary museums.

**How would you say the design landscape
has changed in, say, the last 10 years?**
Highbrow design is dead, or totally
underground, and a rarity in the web ether.
The mass accessibility of the personal home
computer has granddads and grandchildren
with amateur knowledge of Photoshop consider themselves designers. It is a dying trade,
yet saturated with more designers than ever,
everyone knows at least one cowboy - nepo-
tism is tasteless - quantity fore sakes quality
- economic function follows form - marketabil-
ity and the business-savvy override genuine
talent. We battle the accountant as every
contractor is dealing with tighter budgets and
design is the first corner that is cut. It's
ever harder for the upstart passionately creative being to get a voice and enter the professional practitioners' realm without some
sort of privileged backing.

**What would you say is the most distinctive
characteristic of the visual arts in the UK?**
Relentlessly hopeful pioneers of preten-
tious, pompous, pseudo-sophistication
within a plagiaristic imperial mongrel island
mentality - polymorphous pommies.

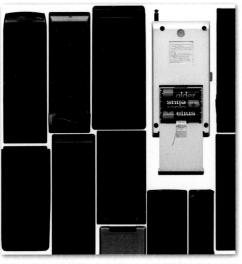
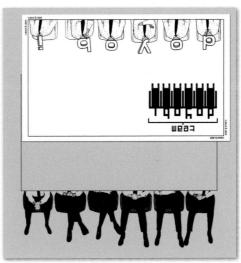

ALDER & ELIUS: PARENTAL GUIDANCE I LP RECORD SLEEVE I 2000

TEAM DOYOBI I CD SLEEVE FRONT I 2001

LEXOLEUM I LP RECORD SLEEVE FRONT I 2001

DJ SIGNIFY – SLEEP NO MORE | LP PACKAGING | 2003

DANGERMOUSE & GEMINI – GHETTO POP LIFE | LP RECORD SLEEVE BACK & FRONT | 2003

X: XYZ Series
Designed By Cuata For Typexco 2008
Curated By YouWasFor/Them/ July 15-20/ Buffalo, NY
www.Cbatta.com

Family

www.designedbyfamily.com

076

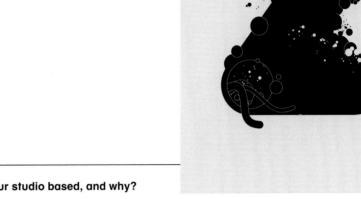

How did you start?
I started out being interested in general drawing, graphic novels etc, this lead onto an art course at school, but it wasn't the thing for me, so this lead on, by recommendation of a teacher, to graphic design. I did a graphic communication degree at university, worked hard as an intern for a year or so, started to work in a local studio and set up Family shortly after as a way to express myself in an experimental print format.

Where is your studio based, and why?
Birmingham.

How would you describe your studio?
I'd like to think strategically cluttered with a hope of one day being minimal

Do you collect anything?
I collect anything and everything print related, Japanese related, manga related, typography related, editorial related…

What are your main influences?
It is a bit of a cliché, but probably anything and everything. As for current designers or studios, I'm a huge fan of Spin, Sea, Hort.

What would you say is the most distinctive characteristic of graphics in the UK?
Not being afraid to push

ALL IMAGES: THE XYZ SERIES | POSTERS

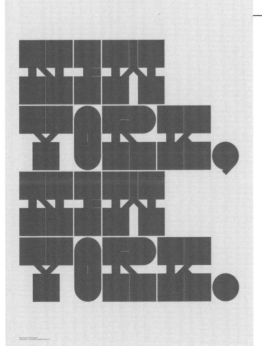

Family
Graphic Design
& Art Direction

Selected Works
2006———2008½

Neue Haas Grotesk
Poster

For the typefaces 50th Birthday
celebrations Family designed and
screen printed a limited run of these
single colour posters.

June 2008

Neue Haas
Grotesk

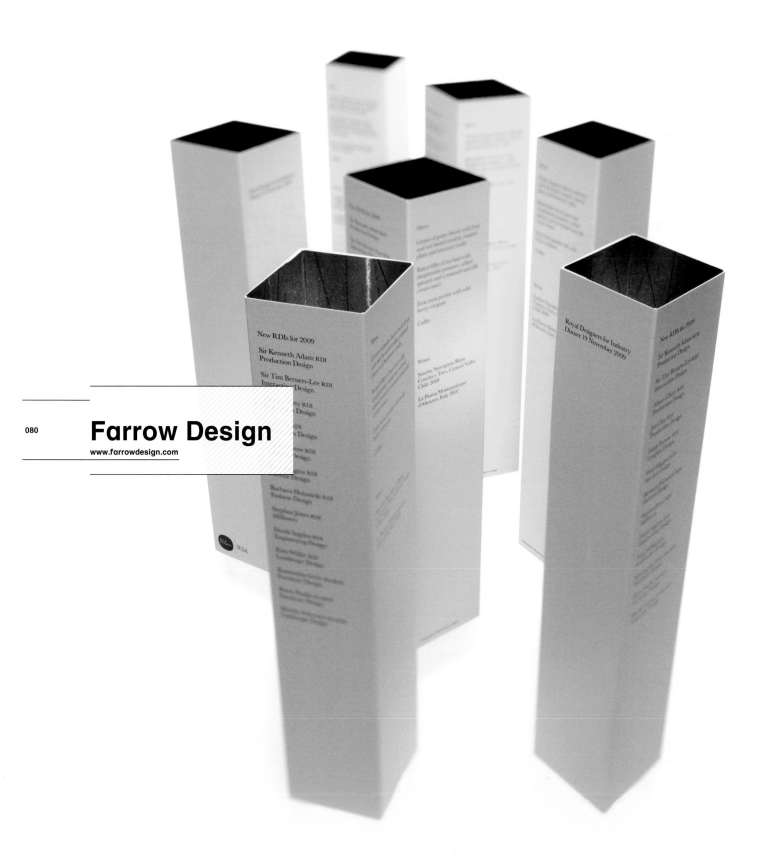

Farrow Design
www.farrowdesign.com

How many people you work at Farrow Design?

At the moment there are three of us: Gary, Sabine and myself, though historically there have been four people. People tend to be surprised by that, as we are fairly prolific for the size of the studio. I'm happy with a small studio.

Do you have any observations about the British graphic design world in the last ten years?

I think British graphic design has been a good place to be over the last ten years.
It will be interesting to see what happens over the next 10 as we enter tougher times.

When did you start? And what type of work do you mainly do?

Farrow Design in its current guise has existed for about twelve years. Our clients are really varied which is very much a situation we cultivate. It's the variation in projects that keeps it interesting; we like a challenge.

Where is your studio based?

The Studio is in the basement of a Georgian house in Bloomsbury, London. We are halfway between the West End and the East End, which works really well, plus there are very few other design studios near us and we like that.

How would you describe your studio?

Very open, spacious and light. We also have a garden, which means we can open everything up in the summer. The walls are usually covered in visuals for current projects and there is the odd framed image on the wall. Not so much our work, rather the images that are part of the given project. We also have a series of black shelves, where we occasionally show off, it is currently displaying the 100 invitationswe have designed for Sadie Coles HQ a contemporary art gallery.

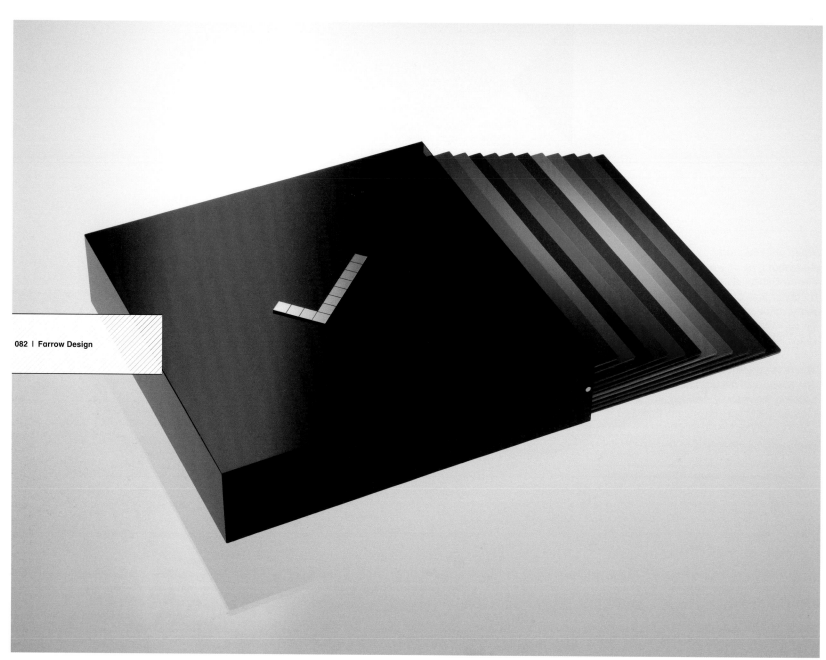

082 | Farrow Design

YES PET SHOP BOYS | LIMITED EDITION BOX SET | 2009

Yes, Pet Shop Boys.

Live DVD and CD
Out now

'The ravishing pop spectacle of the year.'
The Times

DVD Extras include 2009 BRIT Awards
performance, music videos, exclusive live
tracks and Pet Shop Boys audio commentary.

Pet Shop Boys
Pandemonium

Live, The O2 Arena, London
21 December 2009

PET SHOP BOYS PANDEMONIUM | LIVE ALBUM/DVD POSTER | 2010

084 | Farrow Design

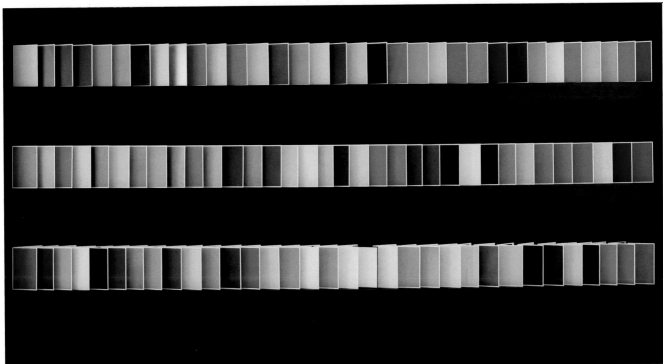

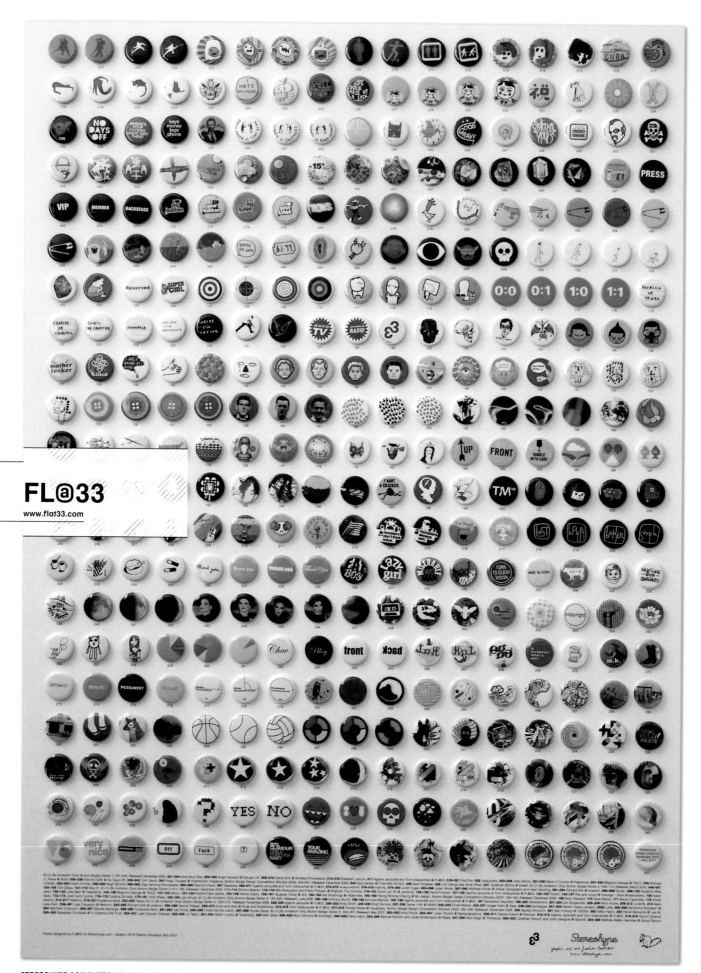

FL@33
www.flat33.com

STEREOHYPE.COM BUTTON BADGE POSTER | 2007
FEATURES THE FIRST 350 DESIGNS CREATED BY ARTISTS, DESIGNERS
AND ILLUSTRATORS FROM AROUND THE WORLD.

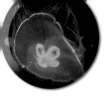

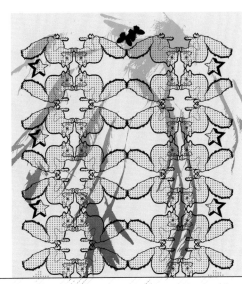

What is your background?

Agathe Jacquillat is French, from Paris, and graduated from the ESAG Penninghen in Paris. Tomi Vollauschek is Austrian, although originally from Frankfurt, and has a design degree from FH Darmstadt, Germany.

What's FL@33 exactly?

FL@33 is a multi-disciplinary design studio for visual communication based in London. FL@33 was launched in 2001 after the two of us graduated from the postgraduate Communication Art and Design Master's class at London's Royal College of Art (RCA). Our first studio in Notting Hill was in a flat number 33... In 2005 the studio moved across town to a larger space in Central London, Clerkenwell, where we still are today. Since 2001 FL@33 won many awards, was interviewed and featured on the radio, online and in over 150 newspapers, magazines and books around the world. A FL@33 monograph was published in 2005 by French Pyramyd Editions as part of their design&designer series. FL@33 are also responsible for the popular and self-initiated online sound collection bzzzpeek.com, self-published trans-form magazine and our sister company Stereohype.com – graphic art and fashion boutique, that opened its online gates in 2004. FL@33 also conceived, compiled, edited, wrote and designed two books (*Postcard*, 2008 and *Made & Sold*, 2009, both Laurence King). *Postcard* was translated into French, German and Spanish. We try hard not to be associated with one or two styles, or projects, or mediums, but instead try to develop new intriguing concepts. It might be more challenging to do motion graphics or a website this week, start a visual identity the week after, then a poster, or a custom typeface. In recent years (and I am aware that this might sound slightly contradictory), we worked almost constantly on books, as designers and as authors. It's probably about 33% of our work at the moment. We love books in all shapes and forms – it certainly is a big passion of ours.

Do you collect anything?

Yes – lots of things, including 4AD releases, envelope patterns, air sickness bags, art and design books (and yes we usually put them on our massive bookshelves). On our walls I see a Supermundane print (edition no 33!), the 'Namibia meets Sweden' poster by Frauke Stegmann and Kajsa Stahre, a screen-printed A0 print entitled 'Destruction' by Megumu Kasuga, our own 'Butterfly contains 818 pencils' print and 'The Italic Poster' by Eivind Molvaer.

Do you have a favourite place where you often meet up after work?

The lounge, kitchen or our roof terrace (with view towards St. Paul's).

How would you say the design landscape has changed in the last 10 years?

The internet changed everything for us and probably the rest of the world. Broadband and wireless connections enable us to work across international frontiers. A lot of our projects are developed without even meeting the client once. This obviously comes in very handy if they are abroad.

What would you say is the most distinctive characteristic of the visual arts in the UK?

The general public here seems to have a much more evolved design awareness than anything we experienced in France or Germany. Generally we experience the British and in particular the London design scene as particularly vibrant and refreshing. One thing is sure though – there's an unbelievably high percentage of talented people here in the UK.

FL@33'S B.I.O.
(BY INVITATION ONLY)
BUTTON BADGE SERIES
CONTRIBUTIONS
FOR STEREOHYPE.COM,
2004–2009

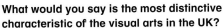

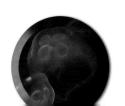

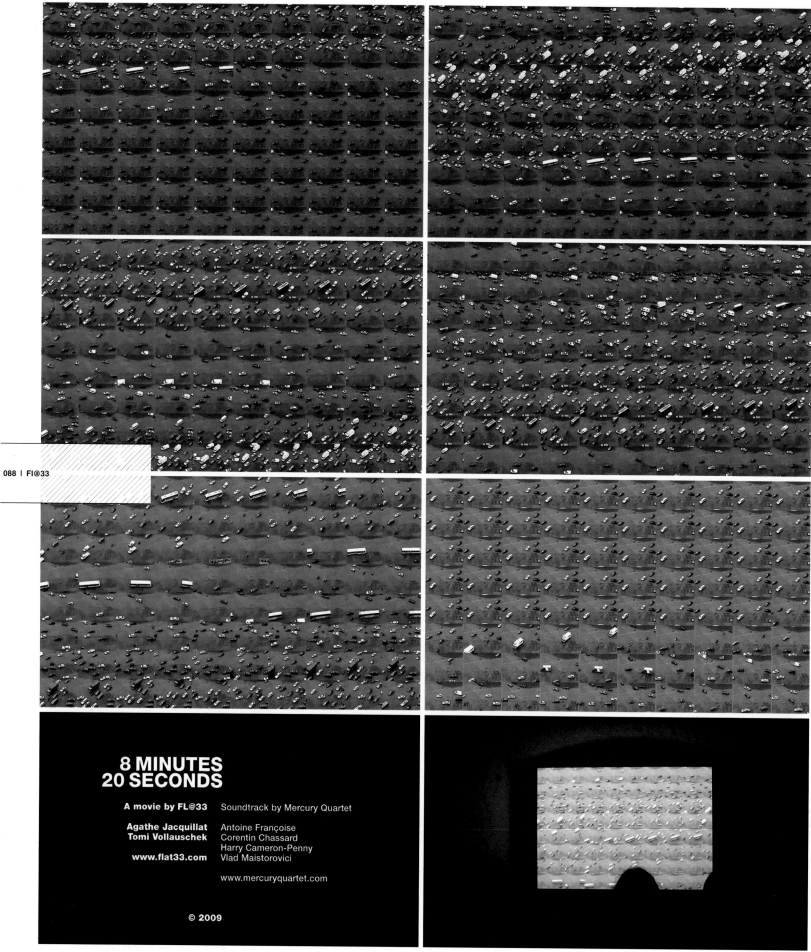

088 | FL@33

8 MINUTES 20 SECONDS

A movie by FL@33   Soundtrack by Mercury Quartet

Agathe Jacquillat   Antoine Françoise
Tomi Vollauschek   Corentin Chassard
                        Harry Cameron-Penny
www.flat33.com   Vlad Maistorovici

                        www.mercuryquartet.com

© 2009

SELF-INITIATED 8 MINUTES 20 SECONDS VIDEO PIECE
2009 VERSION, LONDON TRANSPORT MUSEUM

089

Emily Forgot
www.emilyforgot.co.uk

lust

How did you start?

I studied graphic arts in Liverpool, The first year after graduating was really about finding my feet, I travelled a little and went to Barcelona to gain experience in a studio there. When I came to London in 2005 I worked for a design agency, taking on the odd freelance job at the same time. Now I work on a freelance basis full time from my home in London.

What type of work do you mainly do?

A lot of my work is illustrative, editorial work, book covers, posters, invitations etc. Clients can range from publishing companies, clothing companies, charities and design studios. I like the speed of editorial, but love to be involved in more meaty projects from their inception. The ideas stage can often be the most exciting so working with design companies and other creative industries is always very rewarding.

Where do you work from?

I work from home. The advantage of working from home means that if there is a deadline, I can pretty much get straight to my desk when the alarm goes. I usually start around 9 am, but if there's lots do to I can have a couple of hours work crammed in before anyone has even reached their office. Time defying! On the negative side though, it's often difficult to switch off in the evening and, more often than not, I'm still at my desk at 10 pm or much much later.

What do you listen to?

My partner is also an illustrator and works in the same space… and I often hear his music above my own. It's Noah and The Whale at the moment. I like the radio too, especially if there is a good murder mystery…

What do you turn to for inspiration?

More often than not it comes from the past. I'm currently really into 70's air brush style illustration, but I love polish poster art and anything that makes me smile.

How would you say the design landscape has changed in the last 10 years?

It's so much easier to access information. In some ways I think there is almost too much distraction.

092 | Emily Forgot

LEFT AND RIGHT:
TALL TALES, THICK & THIN
EXHIBITION PRINTS

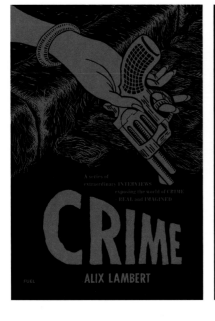

As an artist you look into yourself to understand the human potential to be all kinds of things that are not necessarily pleasant but are real – a criminal, a murderer, a sadist, a rapist.

DAVID CRONENBERG

Director David Cronenberg is best known for his films: *Scanners* (1981), *Videodrome* (1983), *The Fly* (1986), and *Crash* (1996). Recently, he has explored the nature of crime in *A History of Violence* (2005), and *Eastern Promises* (2007).

First memories of crime
There was a famous Canadian gang called the Boyd Gang. I think they were bank robbers. For a kid, that was crime in its Bonnie and Clyde, slightly glamorous mode. And of course, I saw movies very young. I saw a lot of westerns, so there was crime in those. Either Hopalong Cassidy or the Durango Kid would ride out to right those wrongs and arrest those criminals. It was all fantasy and quite distant to a kid living in Toronto. We didn't have a car so we didn't have what I think I got from other people's parents – the idea of speeding. Most early interaction with the police came from cars and traffic violations, still probably does, actually.

The Krays sent me a letter in prison – keep your mouth shut or we' shoot your kids.

BILLY FROST and LENNY HAMILTON

Billy Frost and Lenny Hamilton were both members of the London under during the reign of the Kray Twins in the 1960s. Billy Frost was the twins' d while ex-jewel thief Lenny Hamilton, author of *Getting Away with M* (2006), was a victim of the Krays' violence.

Starting out
Billy: The first time I ever got in trouble was my love for
We nicked a car from outside the cinema, the Odeon in Mile
It was a beast of a car, an old Hillman. We was gonna take it
where we nicked it from. The guy I was with, he said, 'I'l
a drive.' So I let him have a drive. We was at the traffic
at Burdett Road and he put it in reverse. There was a poli
right behind us and he went *bang!* and he backed right it
That was my first time I ever got nicked, I couldn't get out
car. And then after that, you know, you progress. I went it
army a couple of years later.
I hated the army anyway so I went on the run and
when I first met the twins. They was younger than me, I wa
year older. They were about sixteen. We used to go to a c
with them called The Royal at Tottenham. It was like t'
thing'. I met the twins, and we used to have one or two little

Fuel

www.fuel-design.com

BOTTOM: JAKE & DINOS CHAPMAN "FUCKING HELL"
PUBLISHED BY WHITE CUBE | 2008 | DESIGNED BY FUEL
A LIMITED EDITION – EACH BOOK WAS INDIVIDUALLY
BURNED – A REFERENCE TO THE FIRES OF HELL, THIS ALSO
REFERS TO THE FIRST HELL SCULPTURE WHICH WAS
DESTROYED IN A WAREHOUSE FIRE, AS WELL AS
THE BOOK BURNING THAT TOOK PLACE DURING THE NAZI ERA.
THE FONTS USED ARE FROM THIS PERIOD AND THE END
PAPER DESIGN IS DRAWN FROM REVERSED SWASTIKAS.

How did you start?
Fuel are Damon Murray & Stephen Sorrell. We met in 1988 at Central Saint Martins College of Art where we both studied graphic design. We started working together in 1990, at the end of the first term at the Royal College of Art. We were bored with the set college projects so together with two fellow students we started a magazine called *Fuel*. The name reflected our energy and drive to produce work. Early on we began to use vernacular material such as anonymous old photographs, newspaper cuttings and found type like cafe pegboard type or hand made signs found in the street.

Who are your main clients, and what type of work do you mainly do?
The majority of our work is designing books and catalogues for artists and art galleries. (PS: In last few years, Fuel have also started their own publishing house).

Where is your studio based, and why?

When we graduated from the RCA in 1992, we found a studio in Spitalfields in the east of London. Situated on the edge of the City's financial district, there are streets of Georgian houses alongside Brick Lane and the Bangladeshi community. It was this curious mix of people that we found inspiring. At the time it was an unusual place for a design group to be based. The area has been developed over the past 16 years and is now a very fashionable place where many young artists and designers work – too fashionable for us, but we were here first so we're staying!

Do you collect anything?

It's a Georgian townhouse, so it doesn't feel like a typical design studio. Our furniture is a mix of old and new collected over the years – we have an old wooden filing cabinet, a desk made from an old door, 3 old cinema seats and Dieter Rams 606 bookshelves. We display the current books we've designed and the books we've published. There is nothing else on the walls. They are painted white and grey. We have stripped wood floorboards. The music is an eclectic mix on itunes and includes quite a lot of Russian music and instrumental library music. Our studio overlooks the house where Gilbert & George live and work, we sometimes take deliveries for each other.

Who/what are your main influences?

We share a dislike of conventional good taste and prefer things that look un-designed. Other things we like include: vinyl records, cycling and the Tour de France, books and secondhand bookstores, Russia, Spike Milligan, other people's collections.

TOP: ALEX LAMBERT "CRIME"
DESIGNED, EDITED AND PUBLISHED BY FUEL | 2008
THE SCREENPRINTED COVER – LIKE A SCENE FROM AN UNKNOWN CRIME – REFERS TO 1950S THRILLERS, DRAWN USING SCRAPERBOARD TO GIVE A GRITTY IMMEDIACY. THE PAPER USED IS SIMILAR TO A PULP-FICTION NOVEL, AND THE HEADLINES INSPIRED BY AMERICAN NEWSPAPERS OF THE 1940S. RED GUILDED EDGES GIVE THE BOOK A HARDBOILED BUT SEDUCTIVE FEEL. NOMINATED FOR A D&AD AWARD 2008

How would you say the design landscape has changed in the last 10 years?

Over the years, we have managed to blur the boundaries between our personal and commercial work. There are more graphic designers now than ever before so it is vital to have your own voice.

095

FYDOR DOSTOYEVSKY *CRIME AND PUNISHMENT*
**60TH ANNIVERSARY LIMITED EDITION PUBLISHED
BY PENGUIN CLASSICS | 2006**
DESIGNED BY FUEL FEATURING A SCREENPRINTED
DESIGN THAT WRAPS AROUND ALL 4 SIDES
ONTO BROWN CRAFT PAPER. THE COVER PAPER
IS MADE FROM THE SAME MATERIAL AS THE
INSIDE STOCK. THIS CRUDE PAPER GIVES A SENSE
OF THE GRITTY ST PETERSBURG LOCATIONS AND
POVERTY THAT DOSTOYEVSKY DESCRIBED.
THE DESIGN ECHOES THE TENSION AND INTENSITY
OF THE WRITING, THE BACK-COVER OPTICAL
ILLUSION BEING A VISUAL REPRESENTATION OF
RASKOLNIKOV'S BATTLE WITH THE VOICE OF
HIS CONSCIENCE. RUSSIA ITSELF IS A SIGNIFICANT
FEATURE OF THE BOOK, AND WE WANTED TO
REMIND READERS OF THE BOOK'S ORIGINAL
LANGUAGE BY INCLUDING THE TITLE AND AUTHOR
IN CYRILLIC TYPE AS WELL AS IN ENGLISH.

CRYSTAL PALACE

FOUNDED: 1905
GROUND: Selhurst Park
NICKNAME: Eagles

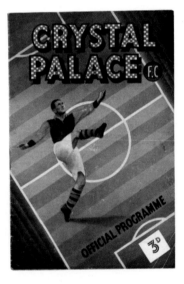

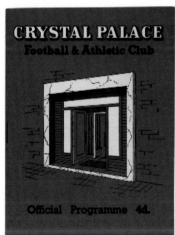

**MATCH DAY FOOTBALL PROGRAMMES
DESIGNED EDITED AND PUBLISHED BY FUEL
2006** I A COLLECTION OF FOOTBALL PROGRAMMES
THAT SYMBOLISES THE GOLDEN AGE OF
BRITISH FOOTBALL FROM THE POST-WAR PERIOD
TO THE START OF THE PREMIERSHIP.

TRUST THE FUTURE

**YOU AIN'T NEVER CAUGHT A RABBIT
(COLLABORATION WITH NON-FORMAT)**
LIMITED EDITION SILKSCREEN POSTER,
'HELLOVON AT ESPEIS' NY SHOW
2007

How did you start?
After studying illustration and animation at
Kingston University I had a year or so of
adjusting to the real world and trying to figure
out what I wanted to do. Luckily, I then
managed to bag myself a job as a junior designer in a small design firm in London.
It was after leaving there that I set up Hellovon
at the beginning of 2006. My work is a mixture of editorial, gallery and some advertorial
work with companies of varying size in the
UK, USA and Europe.

Where is your studio based, and why?
Brick Lane, East London because it's very
near to where I live.

Do you have a favourite place where you often meet up after work?
For a coffee it would be Market Place, and for
beers The Commercial Tavern.

What are your main influences?
This is always such a difficult question to
answer. There is not one thing I can list
as being of great inspiration: from a walk down
the road to a film, ad, image, building, book,
mistake or conversation with my dad could
flick the switch. If I were to narrow it down to
people in the industry that I find particularly
inspiring, it would have to include Non-Format,
Mario Hugo, Emily Forgot, Darren Firth of
WIWP & Six Design, Grandpeople, Peepshow
Collective, Sam Weber, Build and Stephen
Balleux, to name just a few.

How would you say the design landscape has changed in, say, the last 10 years?
It is a glaringly obvious answer, but the inter-
net has changed the industry. Coming
from an illustrator's point of view, this is especially key with regards to the ease with
which an artist can publicise his or her work
and the easy and fast access potential
clients have to that artist. For example, the
majority of my jobs are commissioned without
even seeing a physical portfolio. This has
naturally had a big effect on the relationship
between artists and their agents, as they are
no longer the sole and easiest access
to commissioning an artist. They are by no
means redundant, but it will be interesting to
see how agents adapt over the next
few years to this new climate of endless
artist run showcase folios, blogging sketch-
books, design portal promotion, etc.

What would you say is the most distinctive characteristic of visual arts in the UK?
Quality.

099

2008 I TYPOGRAPHIC TREATMENT FOR XFUNS MAGAZINE I 2008

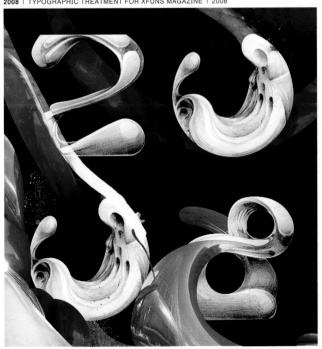

charlton heston

roddy mcdowall

maurice evans

kim hunter

directed by   james whitmore

franklin j schaffner   james daly

linda harrison

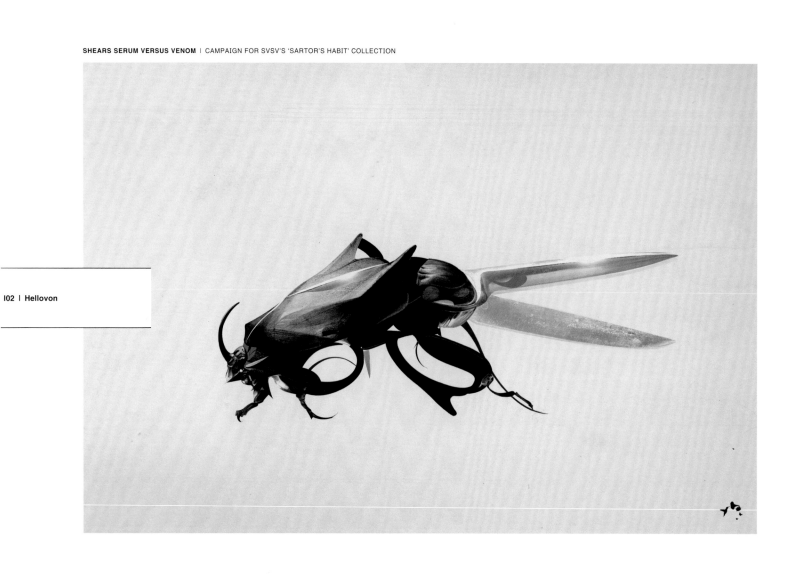

103

Julian House Intro
www.intro-uk.com

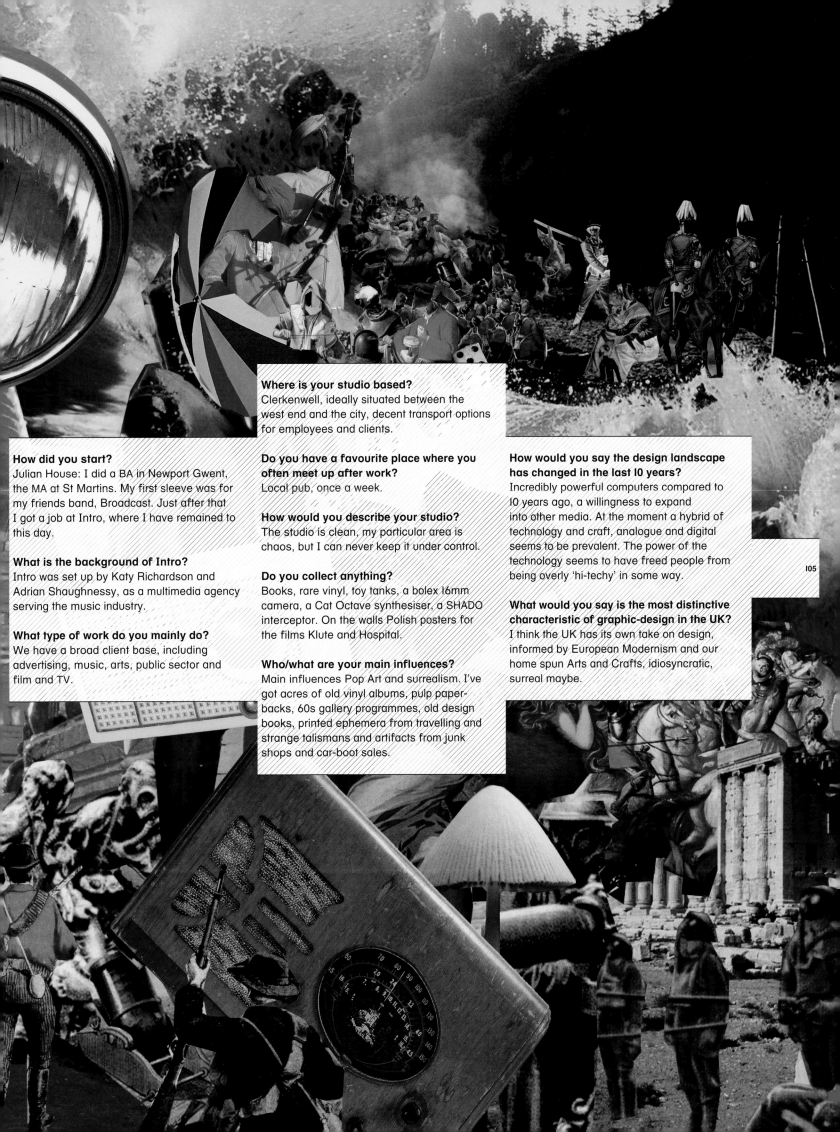

How did you start?
Julian House: I did a BA in Newport Gwent, the MA at St Martins. My first sleeve was for my friends band, Broadcast. Just after that I got a job at Intro, where I have remained to this day.

What is the background of Intro?
Intro was set up by Katy Richardson and Adrian Shaughnessy, as a multimedia agency serving the music industry.

What type of work do you mainly do?
We have a broad client base, including advertising, music, arts, public sector and film and TV.

Where is your studio based?
Clerkenwell, ideally situated between the west end and the city, decent transport options for employees and clients.

Do you have a favourite place where you often meet up after work?
Local pub, once a week.

How would you describe your studio?
The studio is clean, my particular area is chaos, but I can never keep it under control.

Do you collect anything?
Books, rare vinyl, toy tanks, a bolex 16mm camera, a Cat Octave synthesiser, a SHADO interceptor. On the walls Polish posters for the films Klute and Hospital.

Who/what are your main influences?
Main influences Pop Art and surrealism. I've got acres of old vinyl albums, pulp paper-backs, 60s gallery programmes, old design books, printed ephemera from travelling and strange talismans and artifacts from junk shops and car-boot sales.

How would you say the design landscape has changed in the last 10 years?
Incredibly powerful computers compared to 10 years ago, a willingness to expand into other media. At the moment a hybrid of technology and craft, analogue and digital seems to be prevalent. The power of the technology seems to have freed people from being overly 'hi-techy' in some way.

What would you say is the most distinctive characteristic of graphic-design in the UK?
I think the UK has its own take on design, informed by European Modernism and our home spun Arts and Crafts, idiosyncratic, surreal maybe.

105

OASIS TOUR POSTER | 2008

OASIS "DIG OUT YOUR SOUL" | CD AND LP SLEEVE | 2008

OASIS "THE SHOCK OF THE LIGHTNING" | SINGLE RELEASE | 2008

OASIS "I'M OUTTA TIME" | SINGLE RELEASE | 2008

The Willows

The Willows

Belbury Poly

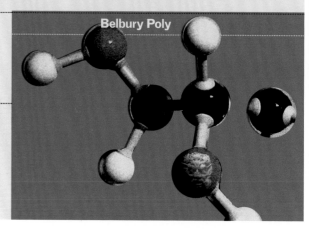

01 Wildspot
02 The Willows
03 Caermaen
04 A Thin Place
05 Farmers Angle
06 Insect Prospectus
07 A Warning
08 Monstroon
09 Thorn
10 The Absolute
    Elsewhere
11 Far Off Things

Written, performed and
produced by Belbury Poly

(C) & (P) 2004 Ghost Box
belburypoly@ghostbox.co.uk
www.ghostbox.co.uk
Cover Design Julian House

GBX003 CD

"It's the sound of their world,
the humming in their region.
The division here is so thin that
it leaks through somehow. But,
if you listen carefully, you'll find
it's not above so much as around
us. It's in the willows." *

"...if this technique is really
successful , the Belbury people
have for all practical purposes
discovered a way of making
themselves immortal." **

* The Willows Algernon Blackwood
** That Hideous Strength C.S. Lewis

Ouroborindra

Ouroborindra

Eric Zann

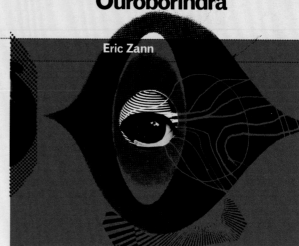

01 It is narrow here
02 Threshold
03 Ouroborindra
04 Dóis
05 The Obsidian Pyramid
06 Voolas
07 The Human Chord

Written, performed and
produced by Eric Zann
(C) & (P) 2005 Ghost Box
ericzann@ghostbox.co.uk
www.ghostbox.co.uk
Cover Design Julian House

GBX004 CD

'Don't you get it yet? It must
work like ... a recording. Fixed
in the floor and the walls, right
in the substance of them.
A trace... of what happened in
there. And we pick it up. We act
as detectors — decoders —
amplifiers.'*

'Inside the infernal box are
impossible spaces, dark screens
and mirrors, terrible traces of
light, calcified thought forms
and endless idiot mutterings.
The switch is thrown and the
magnetic coils begin to generate
their obscene flickering images.
This contraption might have
been conceived by the Old Ones
long before it was assembled by
human hands'**

* The Stone Tape Nigel Kneale
** The Infinity Box Alan Causley & MB Devot

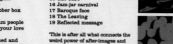

hey let loose your love
The Focus Group

01 Icicle wheel
02 You do not see me
03 Clockbell
04 Echo release
05 Xylophone signal
06 Modern Harp
07 Inside the rubber box
08 Lifting away
09 Today's rhythm people
10 Hey let loose your love

11 String Sine romance
12 The Moon Ladder
13 Planning for urban green
14 Swinging phantom
15 The Thre
16 Jam-jar carnival
17 Baroque face
18 The Leaving
19 Reflected message

Written, performed and
produced by The Focus Group
(C) & (P) 2005 Ghost Box
focusgroup@ghostbox.co.uk
www.ghostbox.co.uk

GBX005 CD

'This is after all what connects the
weird power of after-images and
the strange glamour of phosphor.
The day to day output of this
machine is a synthesis of ancient
dreams and light entertainment.'*

* A Microphone in the Hedgerow MB Devot

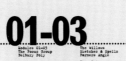

01-03

Modules 01-03
The Focus Group
Belbury Poly

The Willows
Sketches & Spells
Farmers Angle

Hey, Let
loose your Love

A varied program of
musical activities
for educational and
ritual use.

Starts January 2005

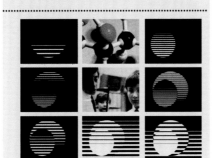

Ghost Box.co.uk

06....

Module 06
The Advisory Circle

Mind how You Go

Timely advice from
The Circle
Remember, electricity can
not be seen or heard.
Harmful, invisible forces
surround us everywhere
we go.

October 2005

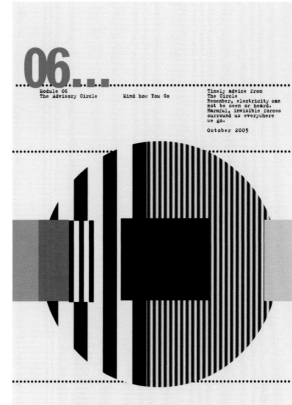

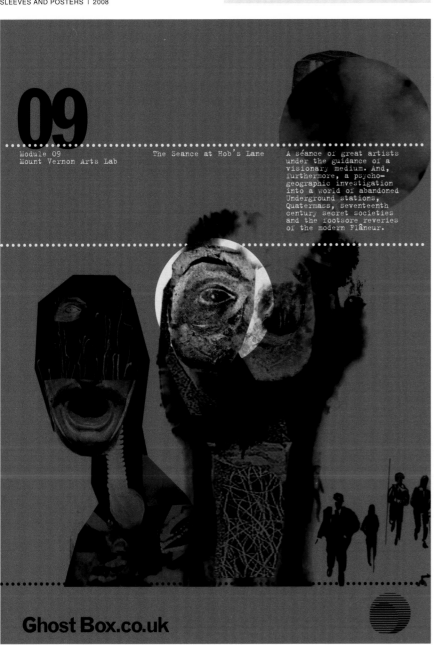

09

Module 09
Mount Vernon Arts Lab

The Seance at Hob's Lane

A séance of great artists
under the guidance of a
visionary medium. And,
furthermore, a psycho-
geographic investigation
into a world of abandoned
Underground stations,
Quatermass, seventeenth
century secret societies
and the footsore reveries
of the modern Flâneur.

Ghost Box.co.uk

GHOST BOX RECORDS IDENTITY
SLEEVES AND POSTERS | 2008

Angus Hyland Pentagram
www.pentagram.com

Erwin Blumenfeld | *by* Michel Métayer

PHAIDON

Nan Goldin | by Guido Costa

PHAIDON

What would be your definition of what a graphic-designer does?
Commercial Art. However, some of what I do has less to do with that and is more aligned to what people now call 'branding' (sorry to refer to the B word). I gained a reputation mainly through my book jacket design, but this now represents only a small portion of my work and an even smaller portion of my billing. I now divide my time up between major Corporate Identity Programmes, Packaging, Exhibition Design, Signage and Website Design and more. I also act as Brand Consultant and Creative Director for two or three clients on an on-going basis.

You seem to have been often engaged in very many art projects (exhibitions, books, etc.) and, it seems to me, almost more as a 'curator' than a designer?
Well, I have never communicated that title to the public. I think in order to be a professional curator you approach your subject with a greater degree of academic analysis. What I have done more often than not is to have exercised my taste or curiosity.

Is there a particular art period or artists in which you take a particular interest?
All the old guys stole our best ideas.

What would you consider as the main points of reference for your work?
Everything under the sun. We all aught to remain open to all kinds of different visual stimulus.

You seem to have been one of the first people to recognise the trend for illustration and publish books about it. How do you personally relate to illustration?
Most of the 90s, when I was predominantly working on book covers, we tended to create and use photography or photo based collage. I realised towards the end of the decade that if illustration was considered so naff it was bound to be due a revival: such is the nature of fashion. Besides, I'm married to an illustrator.

What would be, in your opinion, the next such trend?
Difficult one that. Perhaps, I am a one trick pony. With my consultancy client, Cass Art (art materials retailer), we have been trying to push 'Craft' for the last couple of years. It's the antidote to our digital slavery.

You work for Laurence King Publishing as an art director, what does that work consist of?
Sometimes I feel like I provide a translation service between two different languages. The visual and the literary.

What makes a book cover a good book cover?
Something that intellectually and emotionally connects the subject to its appropriate audience in an engaging and original manner.

How do you see the publishing world today? Do you feel it has changed a lot in, say, the last 10 years?
This is difficult for me to answer with any degree of expertise since I have only ever really worked as an external supplier to publishers. But I guess like all industries where the shift from analogue to digital is so fundamental the change has and will continue to be seismic.

What would you say is the most distinctive characteristic of the visual arts in the UK?
We are dedicated followers of fashion.

III

What were the circumstances that led you to join Pentagram?
Anguys Hyland (Pentagram): It was around 1997 and I had been trading on my own or with a few collaborators for about ten years. I guess I was in the frame of mind for wondering what was the next step. When I was first approached the circumstances were very timely. Did I hesitate? Yes, of course. It's kind of like joining French Foreign Legion. Quite a commitment.

How would you say your life has changed since?
I am ten years older. I have a lot more work and experience and a lot less hair.

What are the upsides and the downsides of working for Pentagram?
Well on the up, you have a unique peer group with the broadest range of design expertise under one umbrella and on the down side you have to work hard to keep up with them.

Are there any budgetary pressures?
Damn right there are.

Guy Bourdin | by Alison M. Gingeras

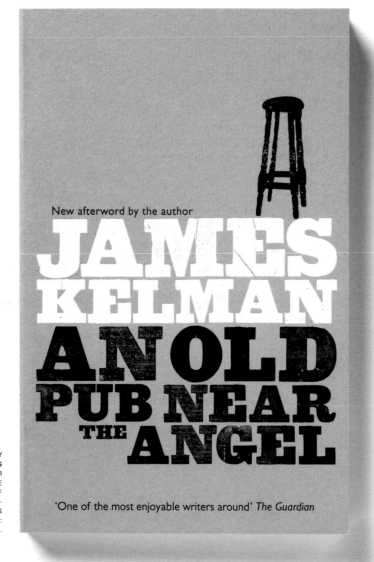

JAMES KELMAN SERIES BY POLYGON PUBLISHERS
DESIGN OF BOOK COVERS FOR POLYGON'S RE-ISSUE OF THE NOVELS AND SHORT STORIES OF JAMES KELMAN, THE CONTRO-VERSIAL BOOKER PRIZE-WINNING AUTHOR. DESIGN ASSISTANT: MASUMI BRIOZZO.

BALLPOINT EXHIBITION CATALOGUE | PENTAGRAM / THE GALLERY AT PENTAGRAM | 2004
BALLPOINT IS AN EXHIBITION EXPLORING AND CELEBRATING THE ARTISTIC POTENTIAL
OF THE HUMBLE BALLPOINT PEN AND INCLUDES SPECIALLY CREATED WORKS BY FIFTY ARTISTS,
ILLUSTRATORS, DESIGNERS AND ARCHITECTS.

iWant Design

www.iwantdesign.com

CELEBRATING WOMEN FILMMAKERS

WWW BIRDS
BIRDS— EYE
EYE— VIEW
VIEW 2009
.CO.UK FILM
FESTIVAL
MARCH
5—13

"SMART, SEXY AND SUBVERSIVE" THE GUARDIAN

birds eye view

BIRDS EYE VIEW FILM FESTIVAL | POSTER | 2009

BIRDS EYE VIEW FILM FESTIVAL I POSTER I 2010

What's your background?

I studied Fine Art at St. Martins and University of East London. On graduating, I spent a couple of years working in record shops and DJing. It was through promoting events and parties I moved into graphics, designing flyers for events I was involved with and record sleeves for the band I played In. I took a job at a printers to get some experience working on a mac. A year later, I got my first agency job at Cog Design. After a couple of years I left to freelance and moved to the Czech Republic before returning to the UK to start IWANT.

What type of work do you mainly do?

We do a lot of event specific marketing campaigns. Album campaigns. But generally, if it's creative or interesting, we will do it. We have designed branding for Japanese music festivals with Paul Smith, Motorbike helmets for Italian bike co. Dianese, album campaigns for Sony, Virgin and a multitude of indies and recently we have designed a range of bags of Italian bag company Invicta. We are currently working with Sony, Tracey Thorn, World Circuit Records, The Royal Borough of Kensington and Chelsea to name a few.

How did you start?

John Gilsenan: I'd been living in Prague for three years freelancing for various clients in the UK. When I returned to England in 2003 I set up the company with a partner I'd worked with for a while in a previous job. We ran the company from the basement of my Stoke Newington flat for just over a year before getting our first studio in an old stable.

Where is your studio based, and why?

We were based in Stoke Newington for four years and loved being out of the main London hubs. Three years ago I had a little boy and moved to Wanstead and had to move the studio to reduce the commute. I wanted the studio to be Central and Liverpool street was easy the obvious. We are now in a beautifully quiet old factory just off Brick Lane. After avoiding the obvious media areas for so long, I really enjoy the atmosphere of the area, it's very alive and full of energy although having Rough Trade East so close is dangerous for the pocket.

Do you collect anything?

Records and music zines and the occasional monkey. On our shelves at the moment I can see some ruby slippers, a Top Hat, 7 bottles of beer with labels designed by IWANT, a scale model of the Mary Rose, mannequin legs with frilly blue knickers, a large gold number 5 and all sorts of crap that needs to be thrown away. On the walls we have paint and an Ed Carpenter Pigeon Light – on the door are Alexander Taylor Antlers.

BIRDS EYE VIEW FILM FESTIVAL I CAMPAIGN AND POSTER I 2008

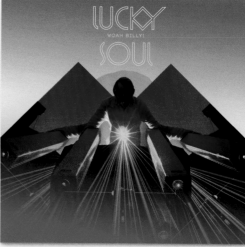

LUCKY SOUL "WOAH BILLY" | VINYL SINGLE

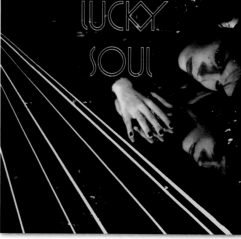

LUCKY SOUL "WHITE RUSSIAN DOLL" | VINYL SINGLE | DESIGN BY JOHN GILSENAN AND HOLLIS BROWN THORNTON

LUCKY SOUL | ALBUM

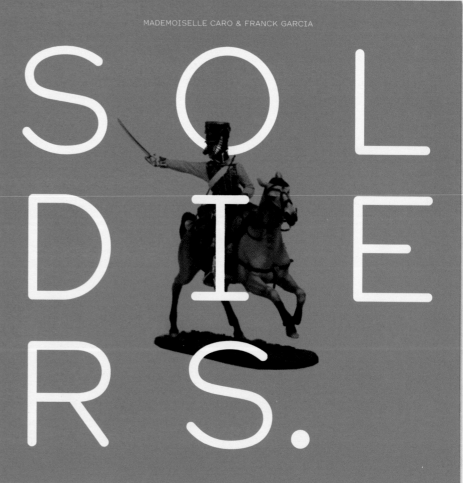

MADEMOISELLE CARO & FRANCK GARCIA "LEFT" | ALBUM SLEEVE | 2010

MADEMOISELLE CARO & FRANCK GARCIA "SOLDIERS" | 12 INCH SLEEVE | 2010

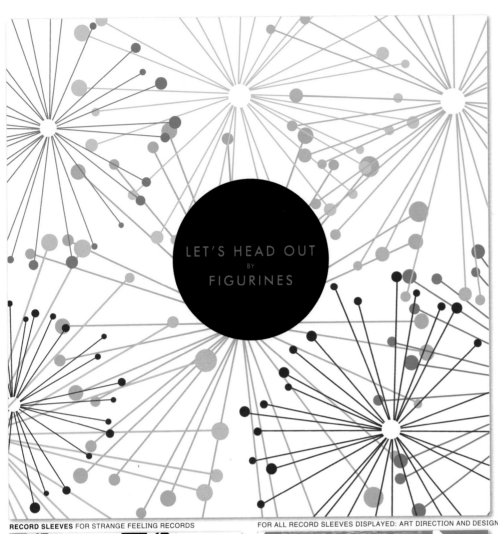

LET'S HEAD OUT
BY
FIGURINES

TIGERCITY
PRETEND
NOT
TO LOVE

TIGERCITY

SOLITARY
MAN

RECORD SLEEVES FOR STRANGE FEELING RECORDS   FOR ALL RECORD SLEEVES DISPLAYED: ART DIRECTION AND DESIGN BY JOHN GILSENAN (EXCEPT WHERE NOTED).

RECORD SLEEVES FOR BUZZIN'FLY

The hole in the ozone
layer has moved

118

Johnson Banks
www.johnsonbanks.co.uk

Campaign against climate change

How did you start?

Michael Johnson studied Marketing and Visual Art, which sounded good at the time, but proved relatively useless. Luckily he began life a 'suit who could draw' at Wolff Olins, before being eventually drawn into graphic design full-time. He had 8 jobs in 8 years, in different parts of the world, making hundreds of mistakes, but learning a lot in the process. Eventually unemployable, he began working for himself in 1992 aged 28, slightly ahead of schedule.

Who are your main clients, and what type of work do you mainly do?

We cut our teeth in print design for much of the 90s, but have dedicated most of this century so far to large identity and branding projects. Many of them so far have been in the cultural/charity/institutional area, and now we're trying to find a few more brave blue-chips as well. We still try to find spare time to do small and beautiful projects.

Where is your studio based?

We used to be in Chelsea, which impressed everyone as an address, but was a pain for travelling. Now we're off Clapham Common, which is less impressive, but much easier to get to. Some of us live south and use cycles and feet, but most of us need the trains.

What time do you usually get to work? What time do you leave?

We're resolutely flexi-time. If you like starting at 8 and leaving at 5, that's fine. Or come in at 10 and go home at 7. Whatever suits, we're not worried. But we're not so interested in that 'all-nighter' macho thing. That's just being badly organized, or not asking for enough time.

How many of you work there?

The studio itself, with part-time admin, interns and placement still rarely gets over 8 or 9 people (most people are convinced there are thirty of us, weirdly). The whole office is plumbed for music, driven from one central system, and we pick from a vast CD collection of many thousands of disks, or wire up our iPods. It's anyone's pick, within reason, although the new Metallica album only lasted two tracks this week. Recently we seem to have been into ambient trip-hop/post-rock/alt-country, if we had to pick out three recurring genres.

Do you have a place where you meet up after work?

To be honest, after spending whole days with each other in a small studio, we don't then spend whole nights with each other that often.

How would you say the design landscape has changed in the last 10 years?

It now seems easier for designers to 'start-up' younger. Everything's obviously a lot more digital, and a lot faster, so we can visualize things so much faster. That has made it harder and harder to justify a decent level of fees though. Paradoxically, the rise of email has meant a lot more typing (not something we had foreseen). We've noticed the rise and rise of 'in-house' design departments within organizations. But it still seems just as hard to break through into the premier league and get your hands on those big, juicy projects. It's taken us a dozen years to be taken seriously.

What would you say is the most distinctive characteristic of graphic and the visual arts in the UK?

A truly vast array of work, styles and approaches. A great big visual soup of stuff that keeps getting stirred up. Somehow all these styles, companies and individuals find work, and stay in business. Who knows how they do it, but they do.

120 | Johnson Banks

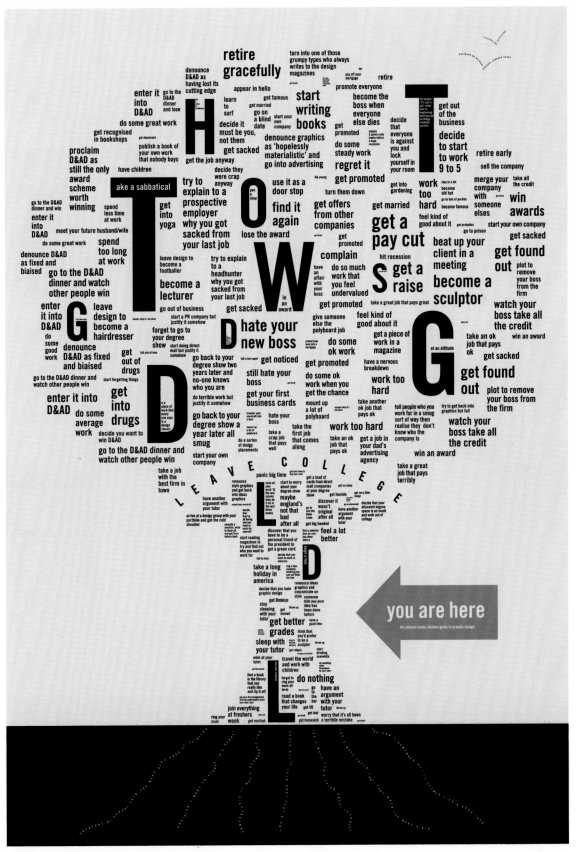

ADVERTISING POSTER

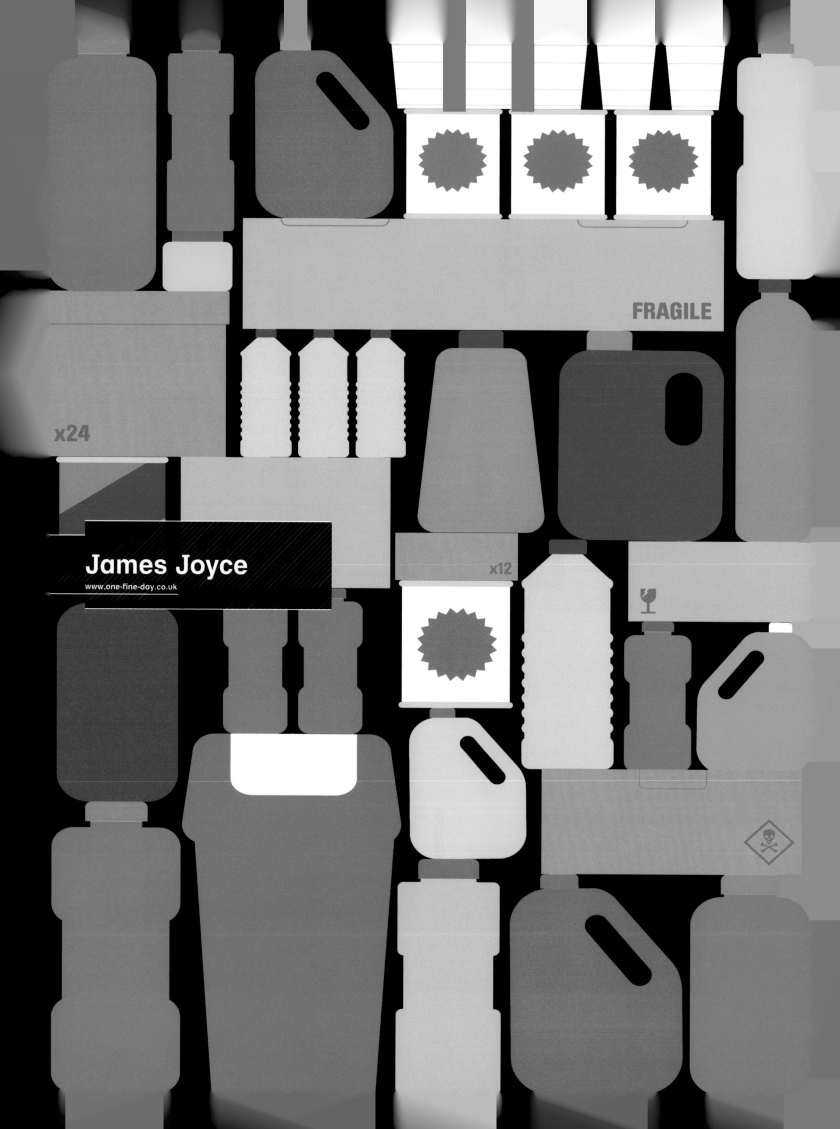

EXHIBITION AT KEMISTRY GALLERY, LONDON | MAY 2008

How did you start?

I went to Walsall College of Art after leaving school and then went on to study Graphic Design at Kingston University. I'd been working as a designer and art director in various design companies for about 9 years. I was starting to get more of my own work in and I was also designing the flyers for a monthly party 'It's Bigger Than' at 93 feet east in Brick Lane. Eventually I had too many of my own commissions coming in so I decided to take the leap and started up my own studio One Fine Day.

LEFT:
CHEMICAL WORLD
LIMITED EDITION SCREEN PRINT
2007

BOTTOM:
WALL MURAL FOR HOWIES
LIMITED EDITION SCREEN PRINT
2007

What type of work do you mainly do?

I do illustration and graphic design, my clients vary but have included Nike, Levi's, Penguin Books, Orange, Kiehls, Carhartt, *The Guardian, Wallpaper** magazine, The *New York Times,* Guinness etc…

Where is your studio based?

I live in Stoke Newington North East London. I get to work on my scooter which is also good for getting around town to do meetings etc. My studio is based in Shoreditch, East London. It's not far from where I live, the studio rent is affordable and there is a creative community in Shoreditch. I share a studio with a friend of mine Dan Witchell who has his own small design outfit called Proud.

What are your main influences?

I always struggle to pinpoint specific influences. I'm interested in work that has an idea behind it, I'm a big fan of a lot of the old-school designers like Saul Bass, Alan Fletcher, Paul Rand, Milton Glazer, their work has great wit and beautiful execution, which appeals a lot to me. Visiting Art galleries can be a great place of inspiration, looking at how different artists approach and execute ideas. I like artists such as Gary Hume, Ed Ruscha, Andy Warhol, Julian Opie, Damien Hirst and Peter Doig. Inspiration can be very elusive, often it's the everyday thoughts, conversations and occurrences that can trigger an interesting idea.

How would you say the design landscape has changed in, say, the last 10 years?

I would say there are a lot more 'one man bands' and very small design outfits around than there was 10 years ago. A lot of the interesting work coming through now is by smaller design collectives and individuals.

What would you say is the most distinctive characteristic of the visual arts in the UK?

There has clearly been an emphasis toward more craft and illustration based work, and a more handmade aesthetic, but then this can often be mixed with some super slick photography or beautiful type and have a completely different feel. If anything I think it's this diversity and mixing of styles and disciplines that characterises the current creative scene.

123

OH ME OH MY | LIMITED EDITION SCREEN PRINT | 2008

We're doomed

DOOMED | LIMITED EDITION SCREEN PRINT | 2008

YOU DO
WHAT YOU DO
AND THEY DO
WHAT THEY DO

STOP TIME

OH OH OH MY

126 | James Joyce

127

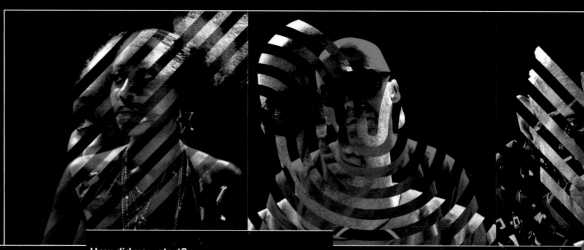

David Lane

www.davidlaneuk.net

128

How did you start?
I suppose I always wanted to do this sort of thing, but an art teacher persuaded me to do design as opposed to fine art. I listened to her. Hopefully, I won't live to regret this decision.

What is your background?
We studied at different universities, St Martins and Camberwell. We actually met whilst working with Harry and Rhonda at Multistorey.

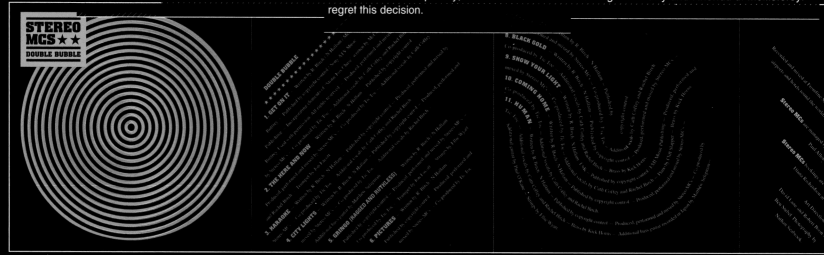

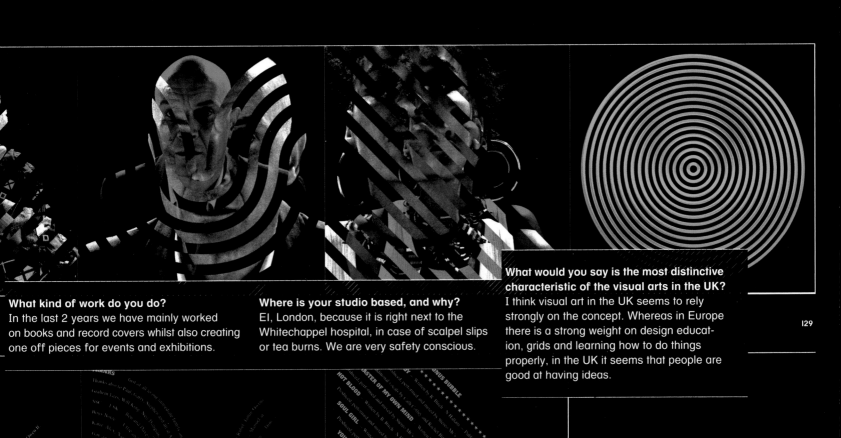

What kind of work do you do?
In the last 2 years we have mainly worked on books and record covers whilst also creating one off pieces for events and exhibitions.

Where is your studio based, and why?
EI, London, because it is right next to the Whitechappel hospital, in case of scalpel slips or tea burns. We are very safety conscious.

What would you say is the most distinctive characteristic of the visual arts in the UK?
I think visual art in the UK seems to rely strongly on the concept. Whereas in Europe there is a strong weight on design education, grids and learning how to do things properly, in the UK it seems that people are good at having ideas.

LONDON STORIES | PHOTOGRAPHY EXHIBITION POSTER

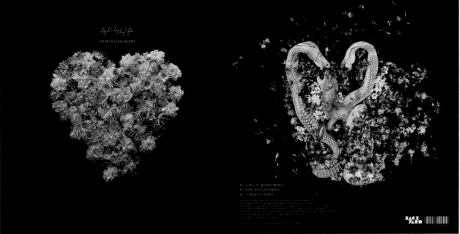

JEALOUS GIRLS: GOSSIP | SINGLE COVER CD J CARD AND 7'' RECORD SLEEVE | BACK YARD RECORDS | 2007

WEDNESDAY 20TH
HEAL'S 196 TOTTEN
LONDON W1T 7LQ

HEAL'S CHRISTMAS/NEW TRENDS/WEDDING&GIFT LIST/HEAL'S DISCOVERS

12PM-2PM   MEET HEAL'S DISCOVERS DESIGNERS AND
JEREMY MYERSON, DIRECTOR INNOVATIONRCA

Domenic Lippa Pentagram
www.pentagram.com

2005 10AM-5PM
AM COURT ROAD

HEAL'S

WEDNE
HEA
LO

WEDNESDAY 20TH JULY 2005 10AM-5PM
HEAL'S 196 TOTTENHAM COURT ROAD
LONDON W1T 7LQ

EAL'S

TH JULY
ENHAM COURT

2005 10AM-
NHAM COURT R

13

How did you start?
Domenic Lippa (Pentagram Partner): I did the usual process of going to art school and starting like everyone else. I suppose the slight difference is that as my father was in advertising. I was aware of what design was from a very early age.

Who are your main clients, and what type of work do you mainly do?
Main clients are London Design Festival, Clarks, Unilever, Edaw, Espa, The Typographic Circle. I work in a wide array of areas, from packaging to print and identity.

Where is your studio based?
Notting Hill. I'm not sure why they chose here – I think it was cheap 30 years ago.

How would you describe your studio?
It's an amazing building, but its also a working studio, and because of this upstairs is pretty messy, but that's good!

Who/what are your main influences?
I would have to say my parents firstly, but then also the rest of my family. I've worked with Harry Pearce for something like 25 years in 4 different companies, so he's still a big influence and I will always go to him either with an idea or a problem. Then there's just a variety of people I meet, from my partners at Pentagram, people I work with here as well as books, films, newspapers, artists, other designers all contribute to how I think.

How would you say the design landscape has changed in, say, the last 10 years?
It's becoming increasingly fractured and people are crossing over disciplines. The old landscape has definitely finished and moved on.

What would you say is the most distinctive characteristic of graphics in the UK?
That there is no rulebook any more. That great work is still done by individuals – whether by themselves or in larger structures – with great clients. The fact that design cannot be so easily categorised reflects the rest of the UK's popular culture – such as art, fashion, music etc. and, as long as this continues and we don't go back to the complacency of previous decades, we will stay healthy.

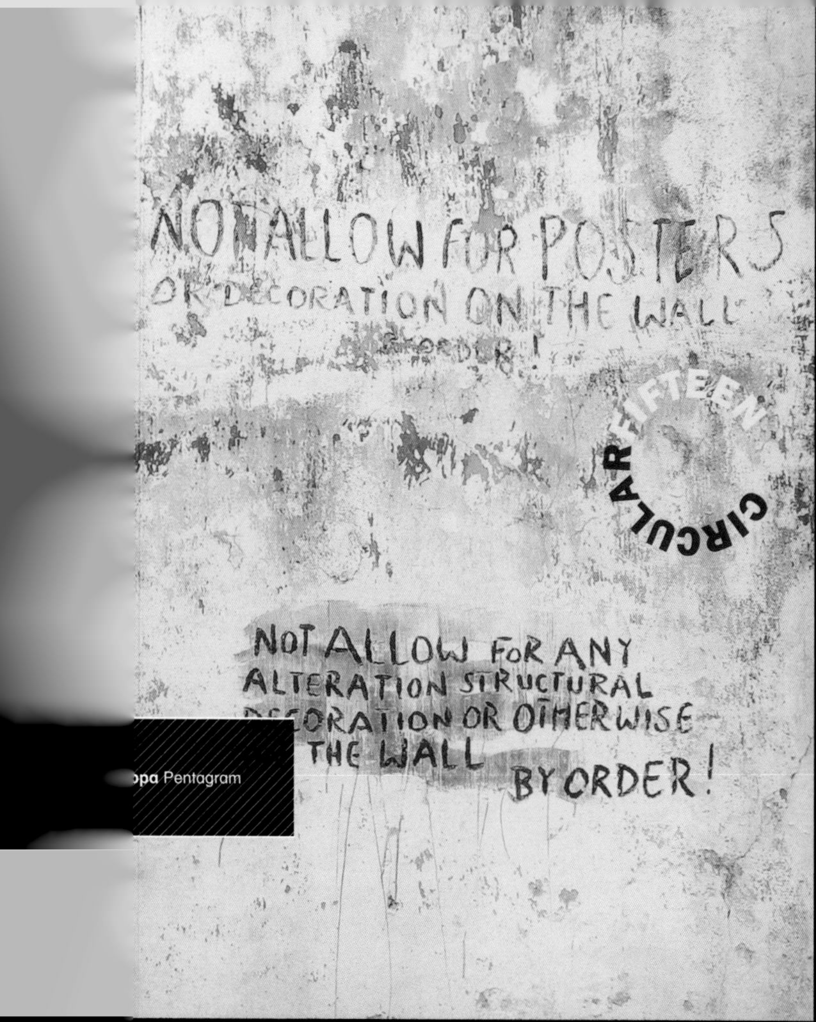

NOT ALLOW FOR POSTERS OR DECORATION ON THE WALL BY ORDER!

CIRCULAR FIFTEEN

NOT ALLOW FOR ANY ALTERATION STRUCTURAL DECORATION OR OTHERWISE THE WALL BY ORDER!

opa Pentagram

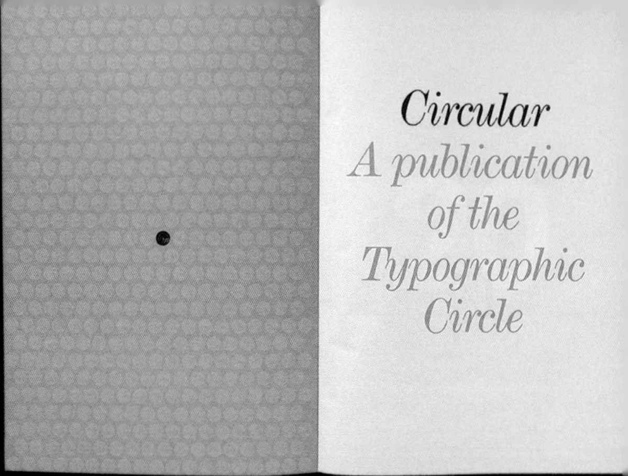

Circular
A publication of the Typographic Circle

15

Y

17

Richard Hollis
Swiss Typography

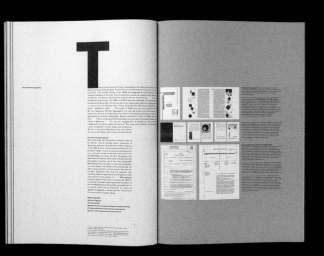

TIME & TERITORY | **J&L GIBBONS** | **2007**
TIME & TERRITORY IS A BOOK PUBLISHED
BY THE LANDSCAPE ARCHITECTURE
AND URBAN DESIGN FIRM J&L GIBBONS
TO CELEBRATE THEIR 21ST ANNIVERSARY.

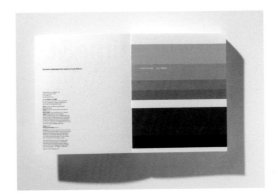

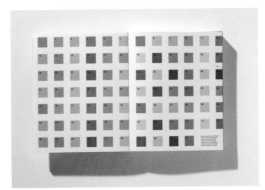

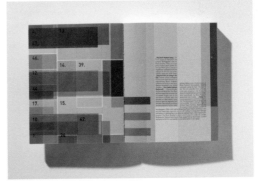

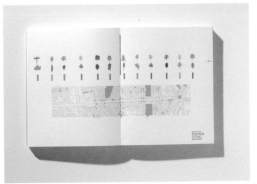

Craig Robins, Ambra Medda
and Nancy Novogrod invite
you to join them in honoring
Marc Newson
2006 Design Miami/
Designer of the Year

Cocktails and Dinner
Friday 8 December 2006
8.00pm

How did you start?
Ben Parker: Paul Austin and I both studied together at Ravensbourne College of Design and Communication in South East London. After graduating in 1996, we both went on to work at North Design. This proved an amazing experience. We worked with some amazing designers. After four years, we felt ready to go off and make our own marks.

Where is your studio based?
Shad Thames by Tower Bridge. It's easy for everyone to get to and it's nice being by the river.

Do you have a place where you meet up after work?
The Kings Arms Pub.

How many of you work there? Who gets to pick the music?
There are a total of seven of us in the studio. Paul and I have given up on picking music – we leave that to the younger guys.

Do you collect anything?
Like all designers, I have a small collection of books, which I treasure. If I find a really special book I tend to buy two copies: one for the studio and one for home. I have a few posters on the wall: an Armin Hoffman, an 8vo and a Vignelli subway map from the early 70s. I also have a Dan Holdsworth land-scape and a Richard Learoyd portrait. These are probably my favourite possessions.

How would you say the design landscape has changed in the last 10 years?
I think the upbeat economy has produced some very decadent and often indulgent design. However, I think the change in the economic climate will help stimulate work in another direction.

139

ESTABLISHED

&

PREMIER

COLLECTION

BARBEROSGERBY /48/ FUTURE SYSTEMS /49/
ZAHA HADID /50/ MARK HOLMES /51/
MICHAEL MARRIOTT /52/
ALEXANDER TAYLOR /53/
SEBASTIAN WRONG /54/
MICHAEL YOUNG /55/

ESTABLISHED & SONS is a British based design and manufacturing company with a commitment to quality UK-based production and an ambition towards fostering and promoting the best of British design talent on an international platform.

ESTABLISHED & SONS work with both world-renowned designers and brilliant new talent, realising their visions with a respect and understanding for each designers individual style. A belief in the significance of these distinctive styles has encouraged a diverse and eclectic premier collection. The advocacy of celebrated designers and emerging names is integral to the company's mission: to build an exemplary representation of British creative excellence.

Proud of our relationships with a detailed network of UK factories, technicians, craftspeople and of our partnership with the Caparo Group, ESTABLISHED & SONS aim to pioneer a renewed belief in the substance and style of British manufacturing.

143

APPROACH

Alasdhair Willis/ CEO/ Established & Sons

'GOOD DES THE USER THE MANU THE BLAC AESTHETI

Raymond Loewy/ Industrial Designer/ c.

Future Systems/ CHESTER

Description/ SOFA
Dimensions/ L2850MM x D1840MM x H700MM
Materials/ FOAM CONSTRUCTION, GLASS POLYESTER
Fabric and Colours/ GLOVE: PALE GREY, DUSK GREY
LEATHER: WHITE, DARK WARM GREY

Zaha Hadid/ AQUA TABLE

Description/ DINING/CONFERENCE TABLE
Dimensions/ L3400MM x D1200MM x H750MM
Materials/ GLOSS FINISH POLYURETHANE
Colours/ WHITE, BLACK

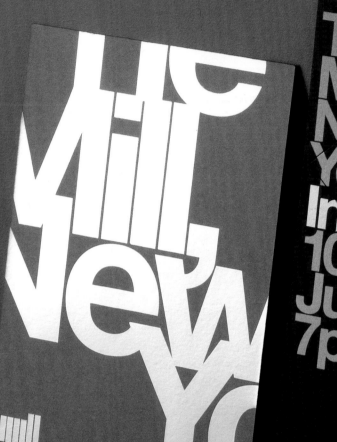

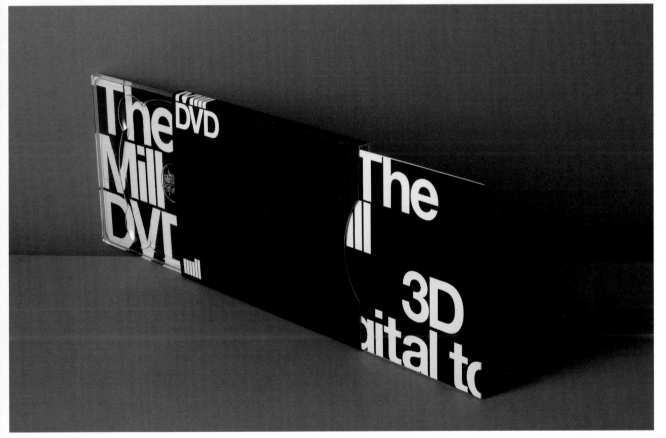

THE MILL | DVD PACKAGING

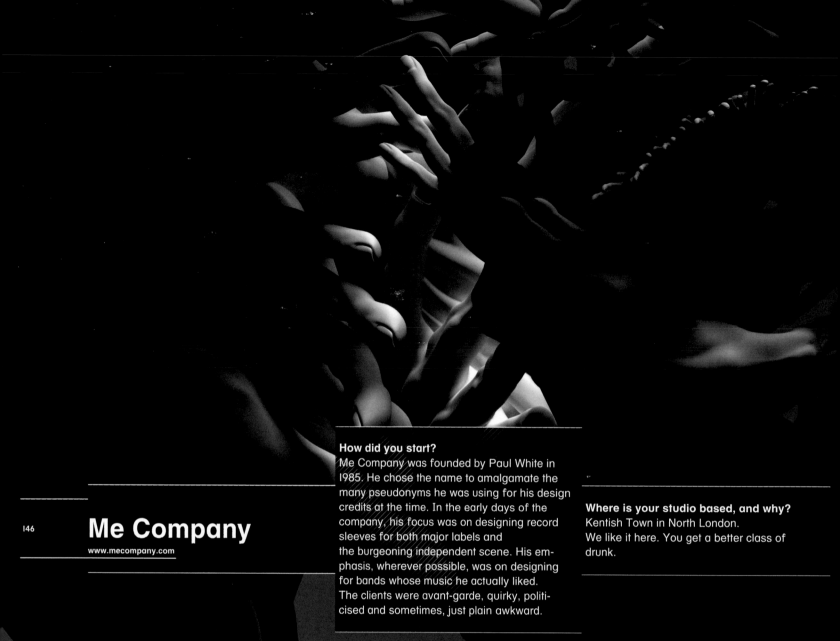

Me Company

www.mecompany.com

How did you start?
Me Company was founded by Paul White in
1985. He chose the name to amalgamate the
many pseudonyms he was using for his design
credits at the time. In the early days of the
company, his focus was on designing record
sleeves for both major labels and
the burgeoning independent scene. His emphasis, wherever possible, was on designing
for bands whose music he actually liked.
The clients were avant-garde, quirky, politi-
cised and sometimes, just plain awkward.

Where is your studio based, and why?
Kentish Town in North London.
We like it here. You get a better class of
drunk.

Do you have a favourite place where you often meet up after work?
The Barbican.

How many of you work there? Who gets to pick the music?
Four people. Music is selected democratically, through a refined form of benevolent dictatorship and motto, "If I wanted your musical opinion, I would give it to you."

Do you collect anything?
Lots of books. A few toys. Some maquettes from days gone by. Ghosts.

How would you say the design landscape has changed?
It's a continual state of flux and reinvention, with the remit far more global than ever before and with the timeline that's more rapid than ever.

PHALENE

MUSK ROSE

Multistorey

www.multistorey.net

SUPER DESIGN MARKET | LONDON DESIGN FESITVAL 2006 | SIGNAGE SYSTEM AND EXHIBITION GRAPHICS

How did you start?
Multistorey is the core partnership of Harry Woodrow (me) and Rhonda Drakeford, with Suzy Tuxen as a designer, and sometimes one or two interns or freelancers. Rhonda and I met while at college at Central Saint Martins. We started going out in the third year, though we never worked together until after we left. Rhonda was quite the swot, and had got herself a job at *Elle Decoration,* I was "freelancing", which involved sitting in the park. I think we first collaborated on a small job that Rhonda had been given, and discovered that we enjoyed working together as well. We managed to get a couple of little jobs here and there as Multistorey, through various people's kindness, and then I became a junior designer at Michael Nash Associates for a bit. Rhonda meanwhile was moving up the ladder, being the one-woman design department at the UK HQ of Aveda cosmetics. I went and joined her there for a couple of months, at which point we told them that we were leaving to set up Multistorey properly, and that they could be our first client. It was a mutually beneficial arrangement, in that we had regular work, and they got us at a good price.

What is your background?
Rhonda was born on a British army camp in the then West Germany, lived there for nine years, then her Regimental Sergeant Major dad was stationed at various places in England, finally settling in Preston, Lancashire, where she feels she is from. I am from London, and have never lived anywhere else. I was brought up in a creative household, going to normal schools, and art college was sort of inevitable.

Who are your main clients?
Some clients we've worked with for years, like the Lyric, or Stærk, and some just appear for one job and promptly disappear again. We try as much as we can to cultivate a very broad range of work, purely to keep ourselves interested, and not stagnate. We've done a lot of print work, but in the last couple of years have been doing more three-dimensional work – exhibition design, interiors and the like.

Where is your studio based, and why?
Bethnal Green. We were in Shoreditch for seven years, but got priced out so moved slightly east. We initially set up studio in East London to be handy to printers and other suppliers, but as time has gone on it's got a bit more fun round here.

How would you say the design landscape has changed in the last 10 years?
There's been a definite change in the last couple of years with the proliferation of design studio websites and design blogs. It's now so easy for people to see other people's work that a lot of design has got very homogenised. Trendy graphics look like trendy graphics the world over. We get sent a lot of student PDF folios, and a lot of the work seems quite impressive at first, as it's very competent, and looks like "graphic design". But generally it's just really boring and not doing anything interesting or new, just aping a current style that they've seen on fffound or something. But saying all that, I don't think the ratio of good to bad work has ever changed from the usual 99% shit, 1% good rule I can apply to just about anything, it's just there seems to be so much more of it generally. The good 1% is happily still going strong.

What would you say is the most distinctive characteristic of the visual arts in the UK?
That there is no distinctive characteristic.

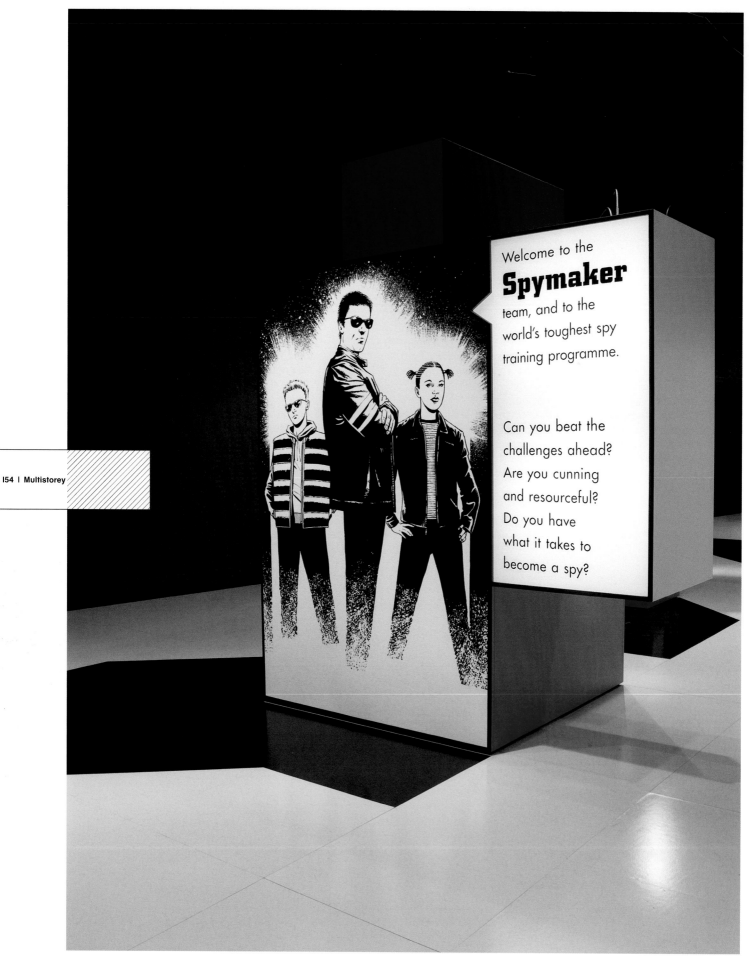

Welcome to the **Spymaker** team, and to the world's toughest spy training programme.

Can you beat the challenges ahead? Are you cunning and resourceful? Do you have what it takes to become a spy?

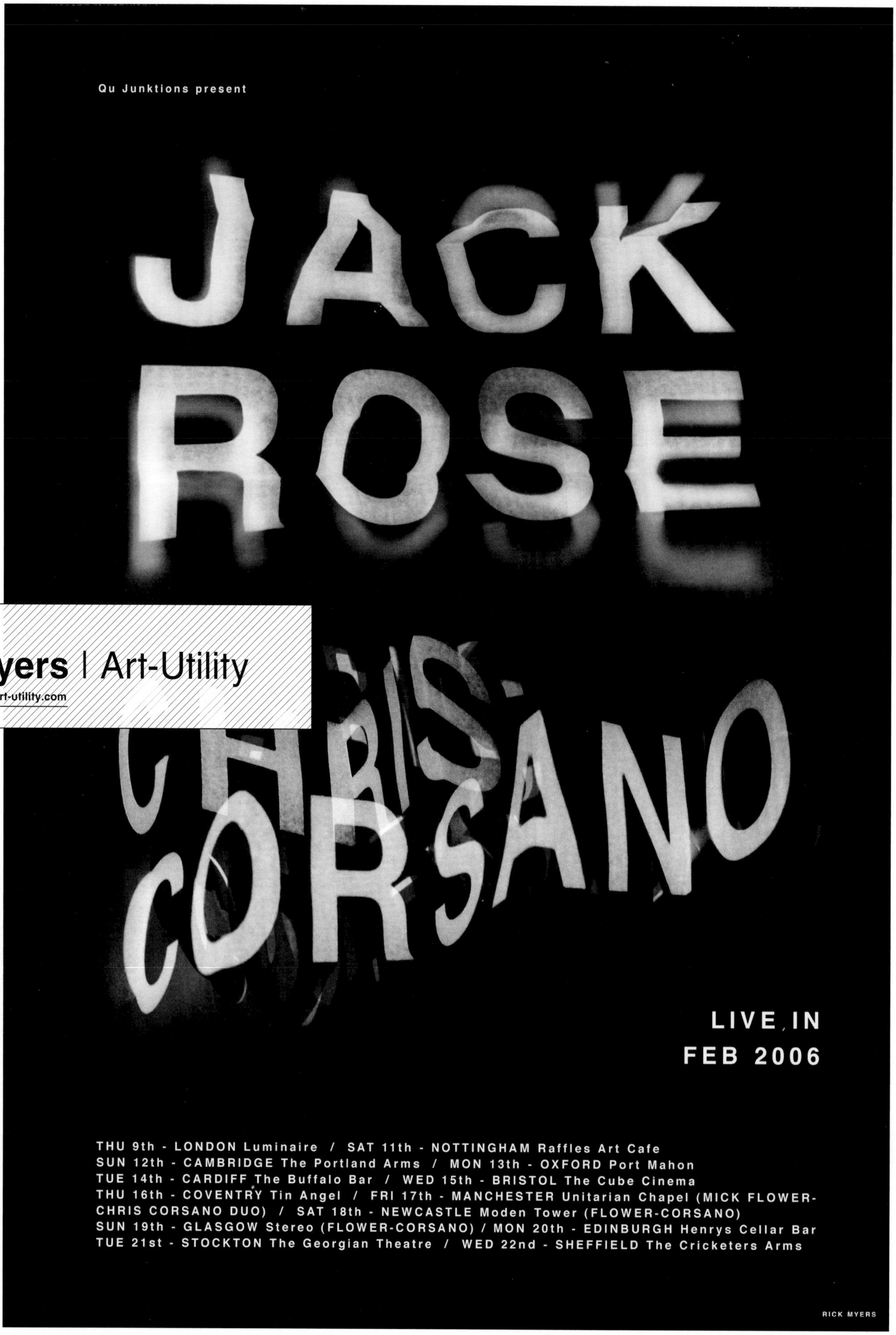

Qu Junktions present

JACK ROSE

CHRIS CORSANO

LIVE IN
FEB 2006

THU 9th - LONDON Luminaire / SAT 11th - NOTTINGHAM Raffles Art Cafe
SUN 12th - CAMBRIDGE The Portland Arms / MON 13th - OXFORD Port Mahon
TUE 14th - CARDIFF The Buffalo Bar / WED 15th - BRISTOL The Cube Cinema
THU 16th - COVENTRY Tin Angel / FRI 17th - MANCHESTER Unitarian Chapel (MICK FLOWER-
CHRIS CORSANO DUO) / SAT 18th - NEWCASTLE Moden Tower (FLOWER-CORSANO)
SUN 19th - GLASGOW Stereo (FLOWER-CORSANO) / MON 20th - EDINBURGH Henrys Cellar Bar
TUE 21st - STOCKTON The Georgian Theatre / WED 22nd - SHEFFIELD The Cricketers Arms

RICK MYERS

CHRIS CORSANO / JACK ROSE
POSTER | 2006

DOVES "BLACK AND WHITE TOWN"
7" VINYL / POSTER | DOVES / EMI | 2004

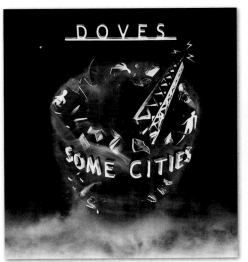

DOVES "SOME CITIES"
CD / LP SLEEVE | DOVES/EMI | 2005

REBELSKI "PLAY THE SCHOOL PIANO"
CD / 7" VINYL | REBELSKI / TWISTED NERVE | 2004

How did you start?
RM: Alone, by building a small landscape with snow and the branches/twigs that hold grapes together.

How would you say the design landscape has changed in the last 10 years?
Environmental problems, regurgitating an abundance of illustrators and photographs of peoples hands holding books open, and hands holding up posters, and things made to look like they're on reflective surfaces – good and original work by yokoland, and more independence than before for many.

What would you say is the most distinctive characteristic of the visual arts in the UK?
Bad teeth

DINOSAUR JR "I GOT LOST / LIGHTBULB"
7" VINYL | DINOSAUR JR | 2007

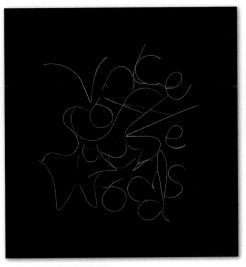

VOICE OF THE SEVEN WOODS
CDR | TOMLINSON | 2008

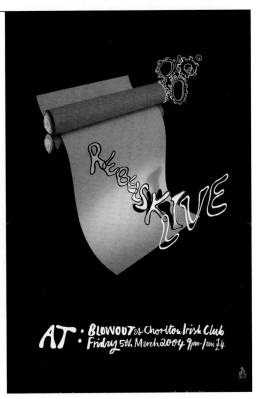

REBELSKI LIVE
POSTER | REBELSKI | 2004

NB Studio
www.nbstudio.co.uk

A PRIVATE VIEW FAY MASCHLER SIMON DAVIS

How did you start?
The 3 partners of NB Studio, Ben Stott, Nick Finney and Alan Dye met while working for Pentagram in the mid 90s. After 5 years and many lengthy discussions in the Cock & Bottle, myself and Nick decided to start out on our own in '97. After buying a flat and a period of freelancing Alan joined us in '99. From the outset we had no clients and no big plan and the rest, as they say, is history.

What is the background of the founders?
Cyan, magenta and yellow.

Where is your studio based, and why?
On London's Southbank, yards from Shakespeare's Globe, Tate Modern and the Thames, 5 minutes walk from Borough Market, 10 minutes walk across the Millennium bridge to St. Paul's Cathedral and the City – need I say more.

What time do you usually get to work? What time do you leave?
It's either an 8.30 or 9.30am start depending on how busy we are. The early mornings are more productive and the journey is more pleasant. Work in the studio ends anywhere between 6.00 – 8.00pm. I often end up taking some work home, but not always doing anything with it.

Do you have a place where you meet up after work?
We usually gravitate towards the pubs in Borough Market.

How many of you work there? Who gets to pick the music?
We are two full-time, plus the odd freelancer and a placement here and there. In theory music is democratic via anyone's itunes. In practice, it is usually hijacked for a few days from the current flavour of the month by a small populist group until control is seized back by the electronic dictatorship, only to be overthrown by an old school coup.

Do you collect anything?
Our shelves are full of the usual books, plus a few rare and special ones, we used to have a shelf for the 'weird and wonderful', but it just became full of junk so we scrapped it. Our walls are usually covered with work in progress and anything that is deemed interesting that week, a letter, poster or newspaper article or random scribble, some end up becoming part of the permanent layer of wall. To be honest, I don't think any of us have ever collected anything religiously, not as adults anyway. In fact, I tend to find obsessive collectors slightly worrying, graphic designers or not, there's more to life. But having said that, I do seem to be amassing project related hats…

How would you say the design landscape has changed in the last 10 years?
It's difficult to say, as you do get wrapped up in your own particular view of it. Our studio has been going for 10 years, so changes we have noticed are a lot to do with size and growth. Early on we found ourselves competing with big agencies, partly because of the fact that we were small and focused, and partly because of new technology and working practices enabled us to deliver like a big agency. The playing field has been somewhat levelled, big agencies have changed, diversified or created networks and alliances. But as the economy looks less stable clients have become less courageous and we are only just beginning to face more and more competition from emerging overseas talent that previously never existed.

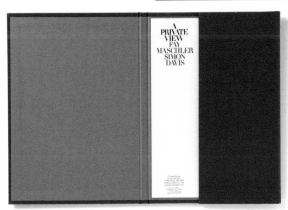

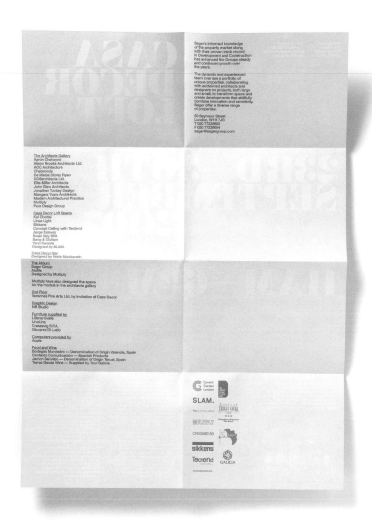

CASA DECOR LOFT
IDENTITY POSTER AND BROCHURE
2007

CASA DECOR LOFT | IDENTITY | TYPOGRAPHIC INSTALLATION | 2007

CHANNEL 4 ANNUAL REPORT
BROCHURE, POSTER, POSTCARD AND INTERIOR
OF THE ANNUAL REPORT 2006

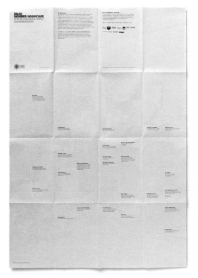

D&AD | POSTER SERIES | BACK AND FRONT

High-level skills for higher value

—

CREATIVE & CULTURAL SKILLS

UK Design Industry Skills
Development Plan
Design Skills Advisory Panel

HIGH-LEVEL SKILLS FOR HIGHER VALUE | UK DESIGN INDUSTRIES SKILLS
DEVELOPMENT PLAN | COVER AND INNER PAGES

Contents

About this plan

Our plan for schools

Our plan for schools

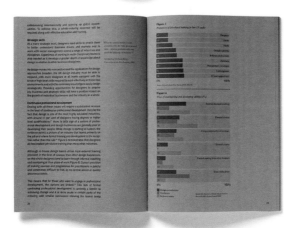

Our plan for the design industry

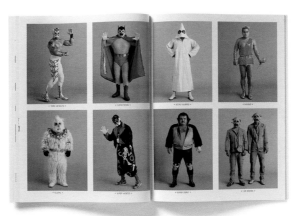

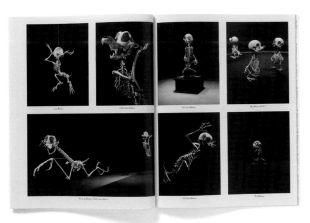

OPEN ALL SUMMER

time to shine.

Non-Format
www.non-format.com

ADVERTISING POSTER FOR NIKE | 2007

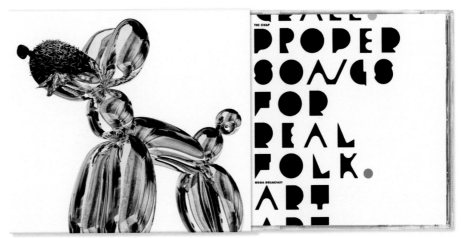

THE CHAP "MEGA BREAKFAST" | CD SLEEVE | 2007

How did you start?
Kjell Ekhorn began his career with a stint in advertising in Norway, moved to London after a couple of years of globetrotting to study for his degree, worked for a few years as a freelancer before meeting Jon Forss and setting up EkhornForss Ltd. Jon Forss studied for his degree in Leicester, got his first job working for an advertising & design agency in Bath and then moved to London to work as a designer for the publishing industry before meeting Kjell Ekhorn.

We started working together in 1999. Our first projects were music packaging for Lo Recordings and the Leaf label. A year or so later we were offered the opportunity to redesign *The Wire,* the UK independent monthly music magazine, so we decided it was time to set up a design studio on our own. We started EkhornForss Limited in 2000 which, after too many confusing phone calls, subsequently became known as, the rather easier to pronounce, Non-Format.

Where is your studio based?
London, UK and the Twin Cities of Minneapolis & Saint Paul, USA. The business was originally based in London, but Jon moved to the US in 2007, to pursue his future wife, and Non-Format has now become multinational.

So how do you get to work?
Kjell still lives in the Old Street area of London and walks to his studio in Hoxton. Jon lives and works from his home in the Twin Cities but plans to open a new studio there soon.

Do you have a favourite place where you often meet up after work?
Tokyo. Until a recent meeting in Dublin, it was the only place we'd met for a drink since Jon left for the US.

Who/what are your main influences?
Pop art. Japanese advertising & design. Contemporary architecture. Modernism. Fashion.

How would you say the design landscape has changed in the last 10 years?
We have more of a global approach and aesthetic. A new idea, or visual approach can be conveyed to anywhere in the world in a matter of minutes.

What would you say is the most distinctive characteristic of the visual arts in the UK?
Although it isn't as institutionally cherished as it is in the Netherlands, the creative industry in the UK is renowned for its constant innovation and progressive attitude. The downside of this, however, is that it can be regarded too easily as being disposable and ephemeral.

167

THE CHAP "MEGA BREAKFAST" | VINYL SINGLE SLEEVE | 2007

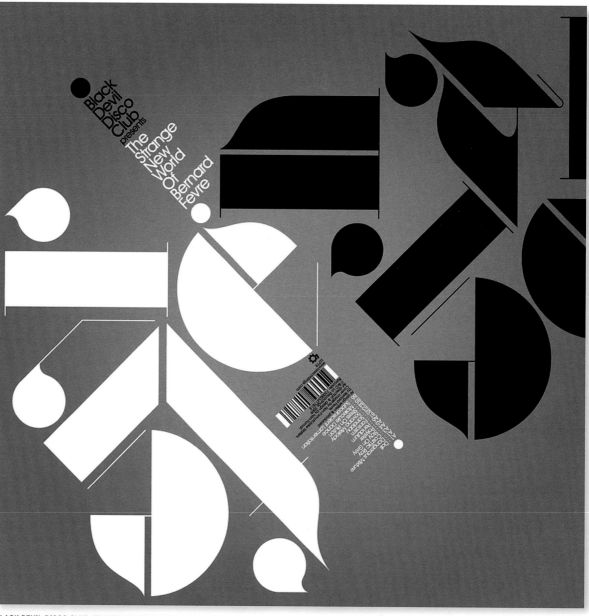

BLACK DEVIL DISCO CLUB "THE STRANGE NEW WORLD OF BERNARD FEVRE" | VINYL LP COVER (BACK) | 2009

169

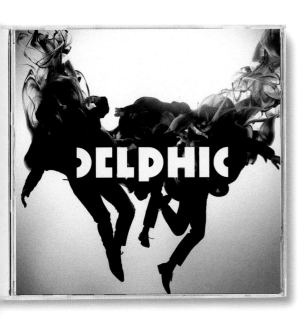

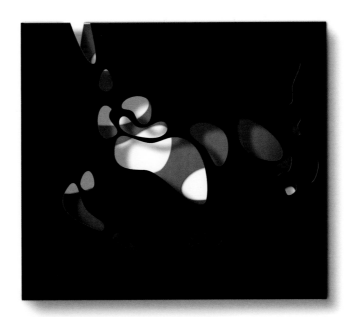

CLARION CALL

DOUBT

...IENTA

RED LIGHTS

ACOLYTE

...

SUBMISSION

COUNTERPOIN...

...

REM...

ACOLYTE

DELPHIC

CHIMERIC

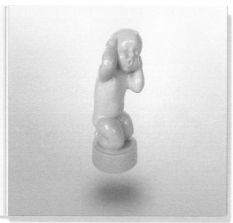

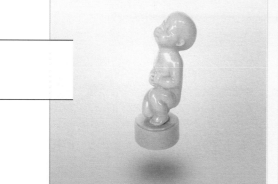

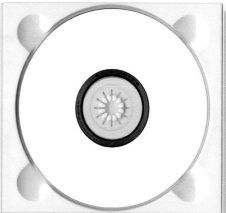

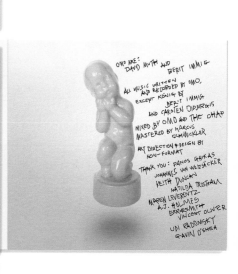

OMO "THE WHITE ALBUM"
LOAF RECORDS | CD SLEEVE
2009

LOAF LABEL MUSIC PACKAGING SERIES

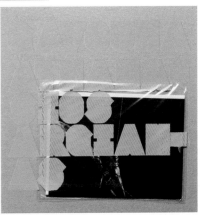

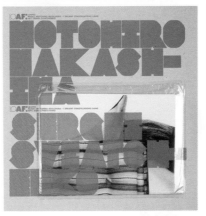

PROMAX: BEYOND CONFERENCE COLLATERAL

Proud Creative

www.proudcreative.com

PROMAX: BEYOND CONFERENCE INVITATION

How did you start?
Proud Creative was established in June 2005 by Dan Witchell. Witchell graduated from Camberwell College of Art. After a brief spell traveling, Witchell spent 3 years in broadcast design, as Creative Director at Kemistry, before establishing Proud Creative. In September 2007, Witchell was joined by new business partner Roger Whittlesea. Whittlesea has considerable production experience in commercials, pop promos, branding and design – with responsibility for budgeting, scheduling and facilitating productions with budgets from 10K to 2 million.

Where is your studio based, and why?
Shoreditch, East London. We moved to our current home when we got too burly for our previous shared studio space. One fundamental goal is being collaborative. Our new space means we have room to grow and contract as required.

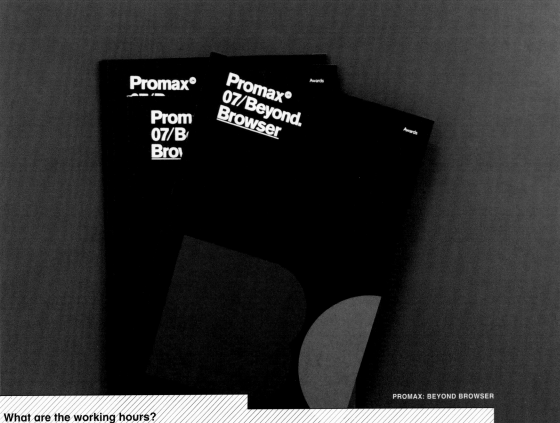

PROMAX: BEYOND BROWSER

How many of you work there?
Five including our resident illustrator James Joyce (One Fine Day), but that can be up-to 8/9 when we are in collaborative mood. Music is very democratic: ipods / laptops straight into sound sticks. Music needs to be fairly laid back or it soon becomes an annoying distraction. Proud classics would include: Cat Power, Beck, Koushik, Nick Drake, Boards of Canada, Radiohead, Midlake, Whitest Boy Alive, Tommy Guerrero and Four Tet.

PROMAX: BEYOND CALL FOR ENTRIES

What are the working hours?
We officially start work at 10:00, but this usually means getting in all coffeed-up by 09:30. Leaving is totally random, some days its 18:30, some days the birds are tweeting and you feel like you've been up all night. We try to make those few and far between though.

Where do you turn to for inspiration?
Without wanting to sound like a hippy, we tend to find inspiration in the everyday, in the mundane and unconsidered – those badly hand painted signs on West Indian hairdressers. In terms of design we always love the work of Herb Lubalin, Josef Muller-Brockmann and Paul Rand from the old school, and the newer ones: Geoff McFetridge, Fffound, GTF, Geneviève Gauckler + a million others!

How would you say the design landscape has changed in the last 10 years?
The college kids are so much more accomplished. They have flashy websites and photograph their work in a very professional manner. That said, you can still see the ones that have better 'conceptional' skills. The biggest change is probably the leveling out of big branding jobs. Pitches are now often small studios against the old guard big agencies. Clients seem to be braver in terms of commissioning smaller studios for big branding projects, which is great news.
Obviously, we think they are right too. They get a much more personal working relationship and bespoke solutions.

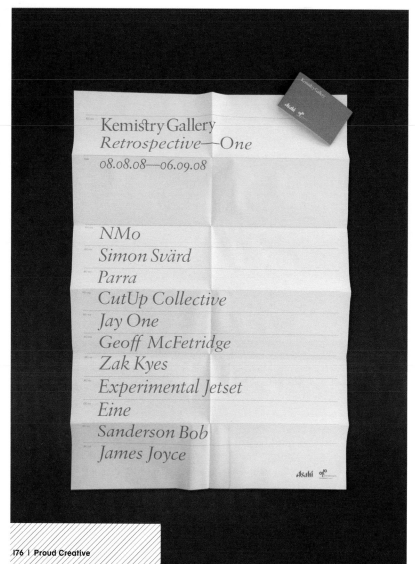

Kemistry Gallery
Retrospective—One
08.08.08—06.09.08

NMo
Simon Svärd
Parra
CutUp Collective
Jay One
Geoff McFetridge
Zak Kyes
Experimental Jetset
Eine
Sanderson Bob
James Joyce

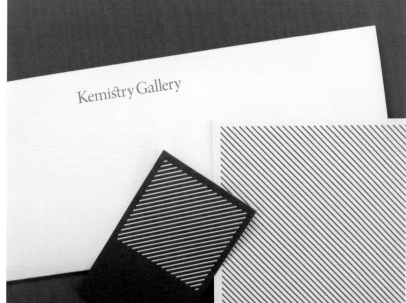

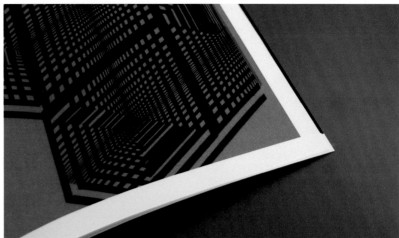

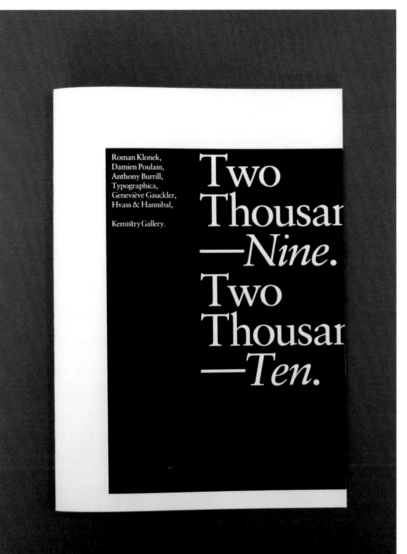

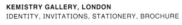

KEMISTRY GALLERY, LONDON
IDENTITY, INVITATIONS, STATIONERY, BROCHURE

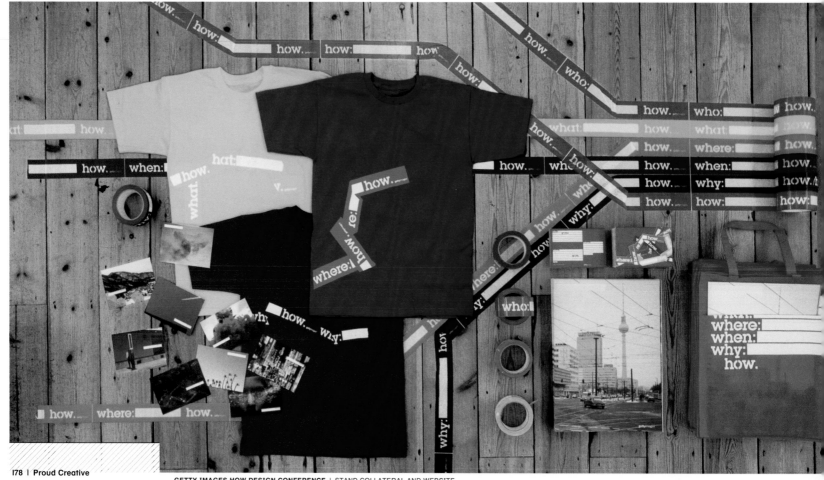

GETTY IMAGES HOW DESIGN CONFERENCE | STAND COLLATERAL AND WEBSITE

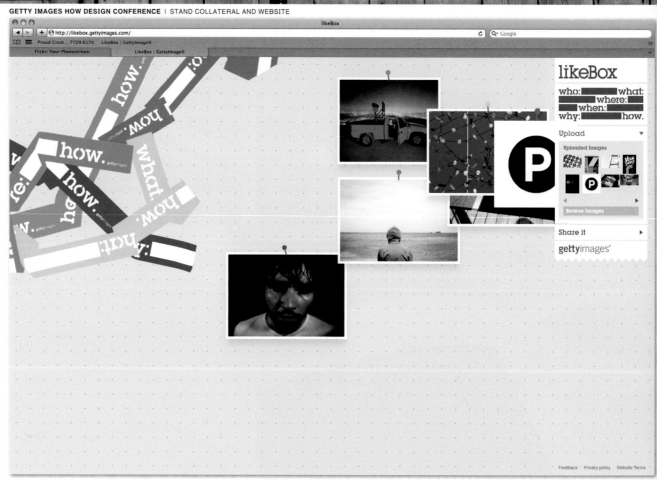

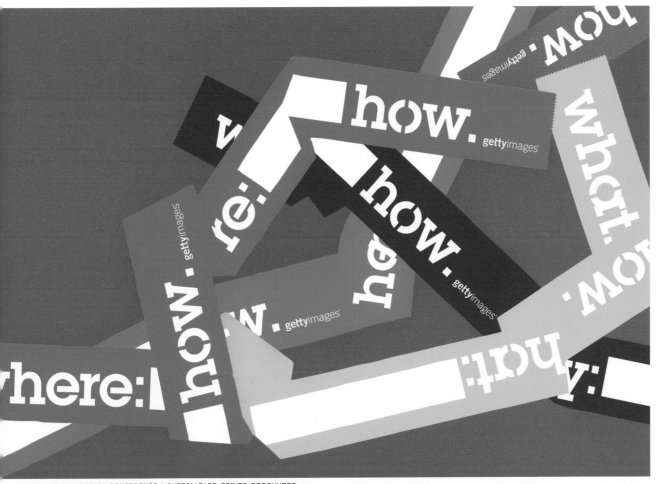

who:
what:
where:
when:
why:
    how.

GETTY IMAGES HOW DESIGN CONFERENCE | CUSTOM TAPE, PRINTS, BROCHURES

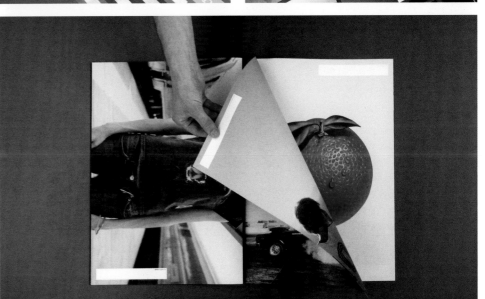

TOP: **SYFY REBRAND** | 3D LOGO   BOTTOM: **SYFY REBRAND** | BUSINESS CARDS

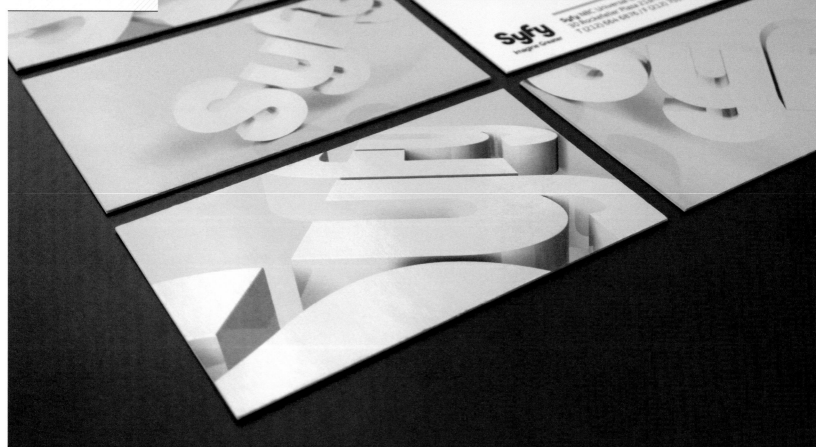

TOP: SYFY REBRAND | POSTERS, ADS

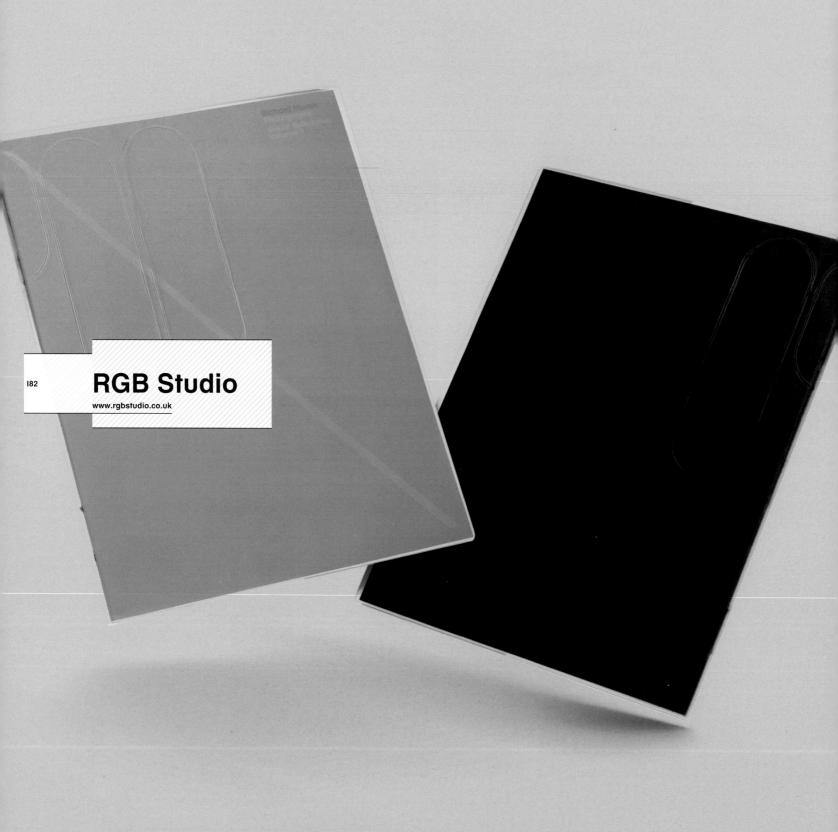

RGB Studio

www.rgbstudio.co.uk

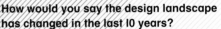

How did you start?
There comes a point in every designers' life
when they consider working for themselves.
It's all about timing, patience and the will
to succeed. RGBStudio has existed for 7 years
as the freelance pseudonym of Rob Brearley.
During winter 2006, RGBStudio became
a recognised design studio in it's own right,
its credentials, built over previous years,
have provided a solid foundation for a multi-
disciplinary design studio.

What is the background of the founders?
Rob began his professional career as a designer at Oyster Partners having successfully
attained an HND in graphic design, typography
and illustration from York College in 1997.
He then moved onto DS Emotion nearly two
years later, followed by Attik, where he
remained for three and a half years becoming
design director of their Huddersfield studio,
working on large branding and broadcast
projects for several global brands. At Thompson
Design, Brearley became the lead designer
for both regional and national clients. He later
moved on again to Love Creative in Manchester. There his role was to lead larger projects
including working for Sony on several Playstation projects including the launch of Playsta-
tion3, and their European software campaign.

Where are you based, and why?
Leeds, UK. Why not?

How would you describe your studio?
The studio falls into the 'considered chaos'
category. Everything is considered as it
enters the room, yet nothing seems to have a
specific place. Until a project ends, desks
tend to be piled high with reference material,
swatches, client notes and unpaid gas bills...

**Do you have a favourite place where you
meet up after work?**
That would be any pub, anywhere.

**How would you say the design landscape
has changed in the last 10 years?**
New, ambitious design companies are
appearing all of the time. 10 years ago it was
difficult to find a suitable role in a Northern
design company that focused on creative output. Today, we have many successful hybrid
companies who are leaving their mark in niche
areas of design on a global level. Work
standards have never been higher, and the
competition has never been greater. It's also a
tough time for graduates. Employers' expecta-
tions increase every year and junior roles have
never been so demanding. The internet has
provided a global audience for creatives to
share their ideas and this has leveled the playing field considerably. It's sometimes difficult
to spot the difference between a graduate,
employee folio, one-man-band and a full service
agency. Illustrator, photoshop, flash, HTML
skills and even consumer digital cameras are
becoming sharper and more professional, making it easier to present work and share ideas.

**What would you say is the most distinctive
characteristic of the visual arts in the UK?**
That's really hard to define. In a country that
has this much rain during the summer months,
I'd like to say optimism, but being honest
it's probably perseverance and arrogance.

"Creamfields was f***'ing incredible ... already etched into the memor of anyone there ... already an instit Melody Maker

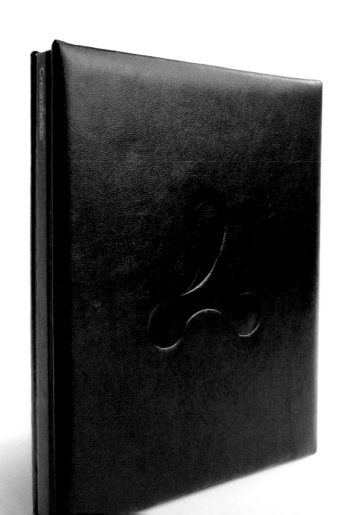

CREAMFIELDS BIBLE BOOK

ARCHITECTURE WEEK
JUNE 15—24 2007
YORKSHIRE'S
URBAN PICNIC

Eat in the street!

Architecture
Week 2007

URBAN PICNIC | IDENTITY & PROMOTIONAL PRINT

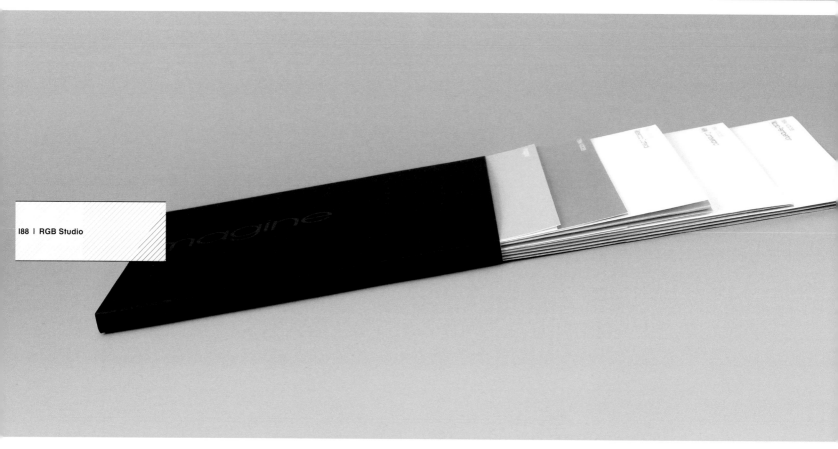

188 | RGB Studio

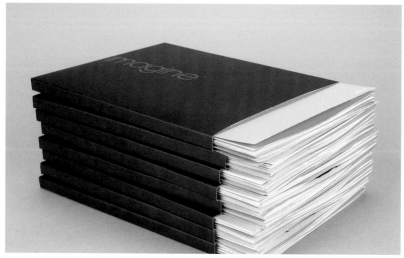

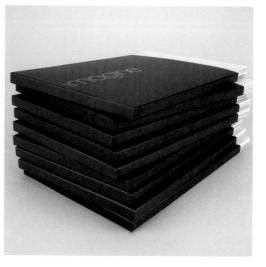

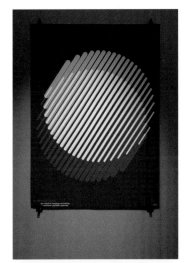

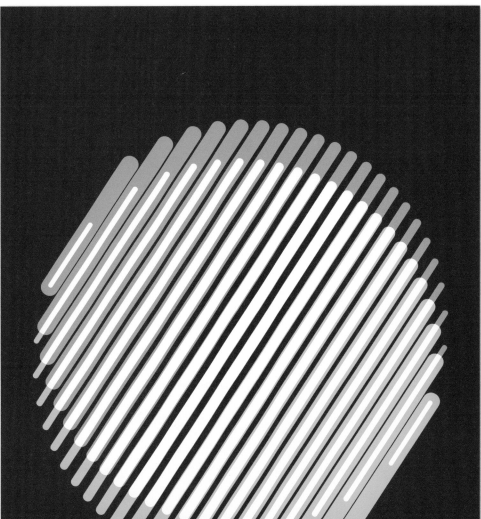

The RGB Studio^c Universe;
the result of merging contrasting
(sometimes opposite) agendas.

RGB.

UNIVERSE | SELF PROMOTIONAL, IDN COMPETITION, POSTER & BADGES

Saturday
www.saturday-london.com

How did you start?
In a flat in Clerkenwell. The two of us. And no clients. It was pretty daunting at first. We walked around to fashion designers and offered our services. Then we took our work to bigger brands. We were young and enthusiastic.

What was your background?
We were both at Wink. Before that we were in Sweden.

Where is your studio based?
Shoreditch. Together with Mother and Poke, we did up our building. The most talented people in our industry seem to like it around here.

What's on your shelves and on your walls?
On our walls is the most recent project we're working on. On our shelves are endless of magazines and books

How many of you work there? Who gets to pick the music?
We're 16 people and the music master is that mysterious "someone", who either happens to sit next to the Music Mac, or who has uploaded the most recent playlist. A guy called Nick, who left us 2 years ago, still controls most of the music, because of his weird underground ambience and electro playlists he uploaded and, for some reason, even though it drives us nuts, it is in the background.

Do you have a favourite place where you often meet up after work?
Shoreditch House is in our building, so we go there. Rochelle's School for lunch sometimes. If not those, then we're happy to come into W1.

How would you say the design landscape has changed in the last 10 years?
More fragmented than ever, between big groups, studios and individuals. An even greater separation between credible design and design as a commercial advantage. The general lack of appreciation from other creative disciplines, which translates into a lack of public money in our industry. The leading agencies have a responsibility to produce work that delivers on its commercial objectives, and still maintains quality in execution and are creatively strong. Easier said than done. Back in the Clerkenwell days, at least the whole Helvetica thing worked quite well. Got a bit sterile in the end, but at least it worked.

What would you say is the most distinctive characteristic of the visual arts in the UK?
There are a few: driven by the work, not about the money, exciting and competitive.

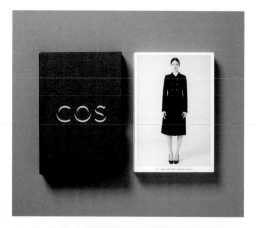

BOOK FOR FASHION
BRAND COS

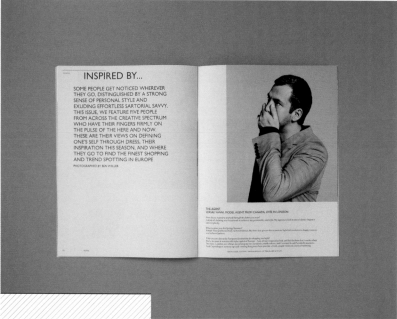

INSPIRED BY...

SOME PEOPLE GET NOTICED WHEREVER
THEY GO, DISTINGUISHED BY A STRONG
SENSE OF PERSONAL STYLE AND
EXUDING EFFORTLESS SARTORIAL SAVVY.
THIS ISSUE, WE FEATURE FIVE PEOPLE
FROM ACROSS THE CREATIVE SPECTRUM
WHO HAVE THEIR FINGERS FIRMLY ON
THE PULSE OF THE HERE AND NOW.
THESE ARE THEIR VIEWS ON DEFINING
ONE'S SELF THROUGH DRESS, THEIR
INSPIRATION THIS SEASON, AND WHERE
THEY GO TO FIND THE FINEST SHOPPING
AND TREND SPOTTING IN EUROPE

PHOTOGRAPHED BY BEN WILLER

A VIEW FROM COPENHAGEN

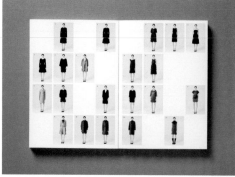

COS | MAGAZINE

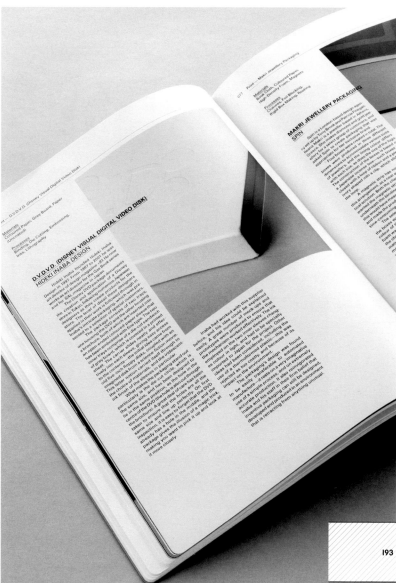

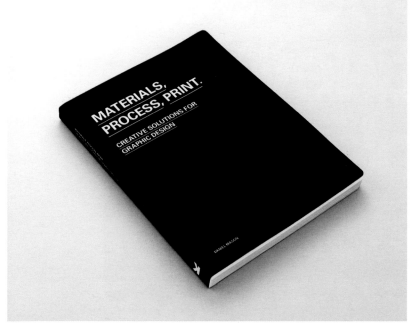

MATERIALS, PROCESS, PRINT
BOOK, PUBLISHED BY LAURENCE KING PUBLISHING

SEA
www.seadesign.co.uk

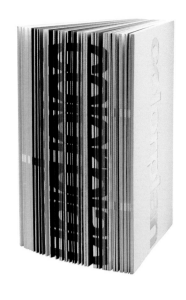

How did you start?
We (Bryan Edmondson and John Simpson) met after we graduated, when we were working for Roundel. After a couple of years we decided that we would like our own agency. In 1996, we began thinking about how to set our own agency up via a small amount of work...
By December 1996, we were ready for a January start in 1997.

What is your background?
Bryan studied at Newcastle Polytechnic and John in Sheffied. Bryan later worked at Imagination and John at Landor, before SEA was founded.

Who are your main clients, and what type of work do you mainly do?
Our main work is corporate identity and Identity systems. Clients tend to stick around. However, we have a mixture of clients at any given time. Right now we are working on an identity for a Gap year organisation, an outdoor clothing brand, and an international publishing group.

Where is your studio based?
It is based near Smithfield Market, London.

How would you describe it?
Clean sometimes, cluttered at other. Our building is split over 5 floors, first floor is for meetings, which is like a laboratory; the rest are working studio spaces.

Do you have a place where you meet up after work?
I like a couple of bars near the studio... St John (which is on our street – St John street!) and the White Bear, across from the studio.

Where do you turn to for inspiration?
It comes from many sources... Architects we work with, clients who push us, other designers work that we wished we had designed! I've always admired the work of Peter Saville, Fabian Baron, Wim Crouwel, Max Bill and Maurice Binder.

How would you say the design landscape has changed in the last 10 years?
The only change is the size of agency. It is nicely getting smaller. Ten years ago, when we set up SEA, the design scene was dominated by large corporate 'brand' sounding agencies. Thankfully these are reduced, or gone – what is left is a vibrant and the most creative community in the world.

COLORPLAN BOOK FOR PAPER MANUFACTURER GF SMITH

BRAND AND GRAPHIC IDENTITY FOR
CONTEMPORARY FURNITURE DESIGNERS KEEN

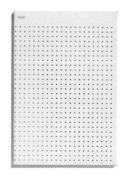

keen

Christmas A New Year
2000

K2 Screen 2006
Edition of 100/Design SEA

IDENTITY & PRINTS FOR 'ART' SILKSCREEN PRINTERS K2

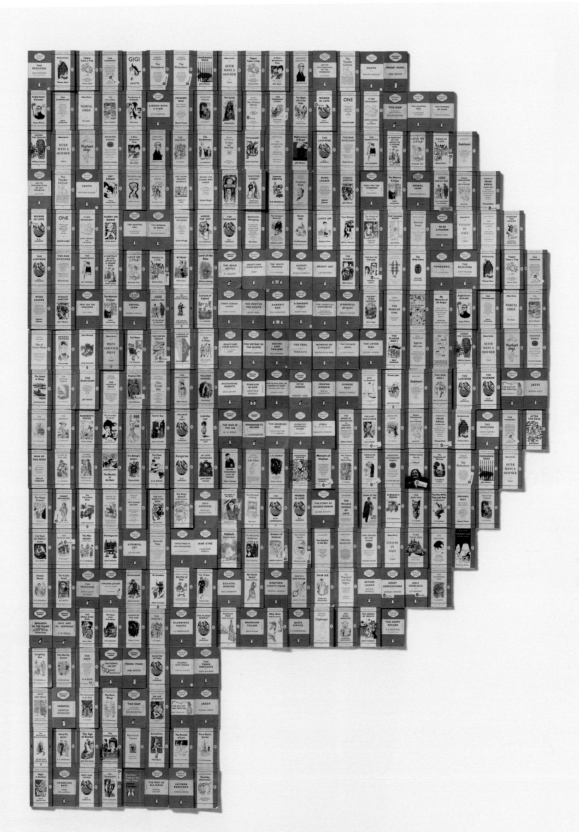

Property of the Public

26 Letters/Bryan Edmondson/Robert Williams
With thanks to Stuart Bailey/John Ross/Sue Osborne/Penguin Books
Printed by Augustus Martin with thanks to David Proud

look
what
you've
got!

Shaz Madani
www.smadani.com

COLLABORATIVE ART PROJECT WITH BILLY WOODS

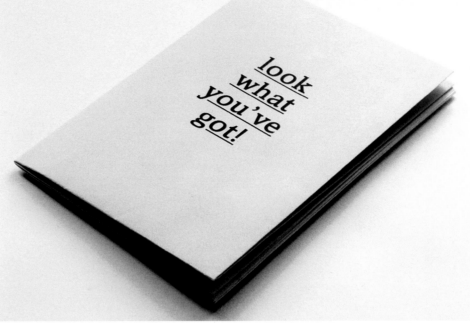

COLLABORATIVE ART PROJECT WITH BILLY WOODS

How did you start?
I've just graduated from uni this summer. After doing my foundation at CSM, I went on to study design for advertising at London College of Communication. Although this was an advertising course, I tried to focus my work more on the visual communications aspect of it. Looking back, I think coming from this background has been crucial in shaping the way I approach my work. It's trained me to always try and remember to strike the right balance between visual appeal and substance, understanding my audience and finding the best way to deliver my message.

Where is your studio based?
One day I'd really like to have my own studio, but at the moment it's not financially possible for me to rent a studio, so I am working from home. I live in a nice little flat overlooking Hackney downs in east London. Getting to work involves rolling off the bed and falling onto the chair in front of my desk.

What are your main influences?
I love design that is intelligent, simple and witty. The work of Fletcher, Forbes, and Gill, is always a source of inspiration to me, and I firmly believe in their motto that "solutions ought to derive from the subject matter; that the designer should therefore have no preconceived graphic styles".

What would you say is the most distinctive characteristic of graphic and the visual arts in the UK?
Emm... I think designers from the UK offer more thoughtful and concept driven design, which is also often much more experimental and fresh.

THE GUIDE TO UNCOATED PAPER

MAN OR MOUSE? READ A GOOD BOOK. GO FOR A BIKE RIDE. PLAY WITH THE KIDS.
WALK THE DOG. BUILD A MODEL PLANE. TAKE UP A NEW HOBBY.
BAKE A CAKE. ENJOY MORE OF WHAT YOU CAN'T DO ONLINE.

GO OFFLINE TODAY.

MAN OR MOUSE, A CAMPAIGN
DEVISED TO ENCOURAGE INTERNET USERS TO
CUT DOWN ON THEIR TIME ON THE WEB
AND ENJOY MORE OF THE PHYSICAL WORLD

MAN OR MOUSE, A CAMPAIGN
POSTERS LETTERPRESSED BY HAND

UNLINE

STARE AT THE MONITOR ALL DAY, THEN GO HOME AND STARE AT THE MONITOR ALL NIGHT..

TOOTHPASTE IS POINTLESS
POSTERS

TOOTHPASTE IS POINTLESS HAVE AN APPLE INSTEAD

BRUSH ING TEETH EVERY DAY

MORNINGS & EVENINGS

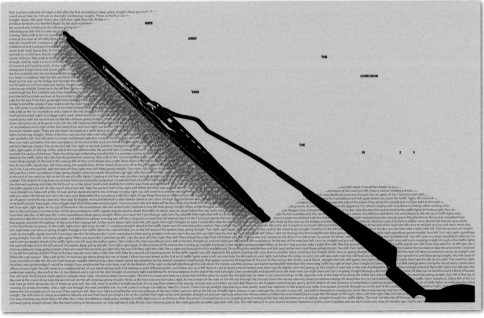

WIPE AWAY THE CONFUSION TAKE THE M25

YOUR JOURNEY MADE SIMPLE
RESPONSE DESIGNED TO PROMOTE THE M25 MOTORWAY, THE REVERSE SIDE READS:
"WIPE AWAY THE CONFUSION TAKE THE M25"

LONG LUNCH POSTER FOR SPIN TALK
CLIENT: LONG LUNCH
SCREEN-PRINTED ONTO PROOFS FROM
PREVIOUS SPIN JOBS | 2007

Spin
www.spin.co.uk

How did you start?
We set up in 1992 in the spare bedroom of
a 2-bedroom flat in Streatham, South London.
The UK was in recession and we weren't in
a position to be too choosy about what work
we took on.

What's your background?
Tony Brook was trained as a designer,
attending College in Halifax, West Yorkshire
and Taunton, Somerset. He worked in
the record industry as a designer before Spin.
Patricia Finegan was trained in fashion
management and worked in fashion PR
before setting up Spin.

**Who are your main clients, and what type
of work do you mainly do?**
Our primary source of work is identity design,
within this area we work in print, motion
graphics and new media. Our client base is
very diverse.

Where is your studio based?
We are in Kennington, South London,
very near to the Oval Cricket Ground. It is
fairly close to home and Tony loves
Cricket!

**Do you have a place where you meet
up after work?**
There is a quite traditional pub in a very
genteel square around the corner called
The Prince of Wales that we frequent.

**How would you describe your studio?
Clean? Cluttered? Improvised? Carefully
thought-out?**
It is all of those things at various times,
there is a carefully thought out structure which
underpins the studio and allows to be clean
or chaotic.

Do you collect anything?
We all collect posters and design books.
We have posters and run-outs from our current
projects on the walls.

**How would you say the design landscape
has changed in the last 10 years?**
10 years ago much of the design in the UK
was a technologically inspired mess. It seems
designers are much more in control of
now, a real sense of purpose and control is
returning and the quality is very big.

**What would you say is the most distinctive
characteristic of the visual arts in the UK?**
There are a lot of fantastic boutique studios
now, with a huge range of opinions and ex-
pressions, the UK scene is much harder
to pigeonhole now than it has been in the past
and is much better for it.

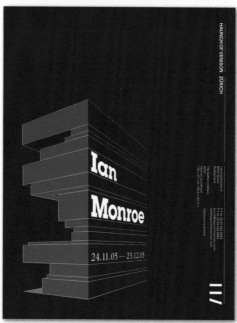

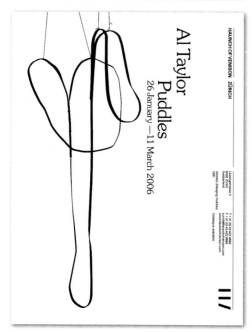

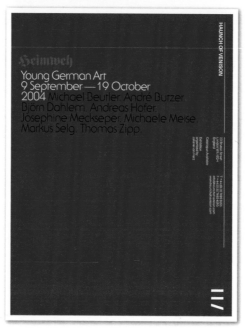

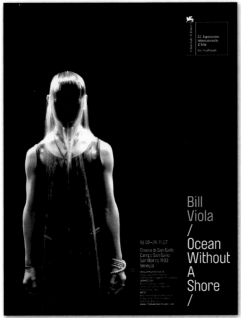

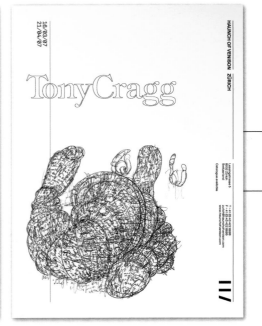

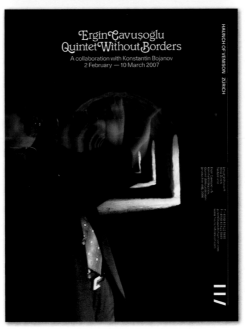

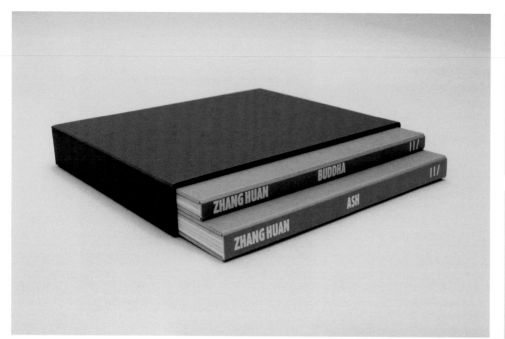

ZHANG HUAN CATALOGUE
HAUNCH OF VENISON GALLERY
CASE BOUND WITH FLUSH
CUT COVERS.
WHITE FOIL BLOCKING.
2007

ZHANG HUAN INVITE
HAUNCH OF VENISON GALLERY
FOIL BLOCKED GREY
BOARD WITH TIP ON STICKER.
2007

KEITH TYSON
NATURE PAINTINGS CATALOGUE
HAUNCH OF VENISON GALLERY
CASE BOUND IN PADDED
LEATHER WITH GOLD FOILING.
2007

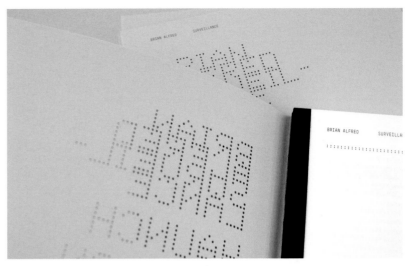

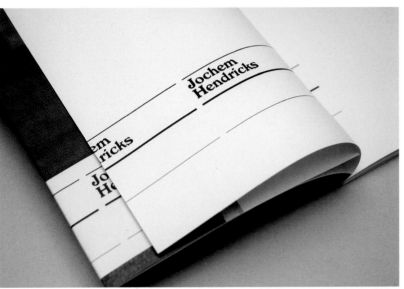

JOCHEM HENDRICKS CATALOGUE
HAUNCH OF VENISON GALLERY
8 PAGE COVER WITH WRAP-AROUND
STICKER | 2007

JORGE PARDO
HAUNCH OF VENISON GALLERY
EXPOSED BIND WITH
CUSTOM-MADE PLASTIC JACKET.
2005

OWNING ART
CULTURE SHOCK MEDIA
CASE BOUND IN LINEN
WITH WHITE &
BROWN FOIL BLOCKING.
2006

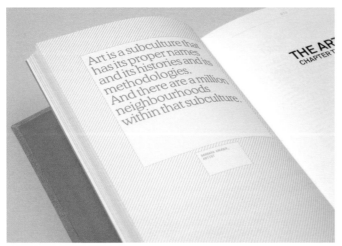

MATTHEW HILTON IDENTITY
WEBSITE & LITHO PRINTED
FOLDED PROMOTIONAL POSTER.
2007

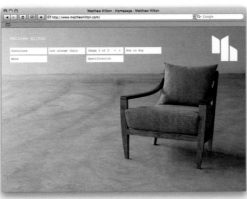

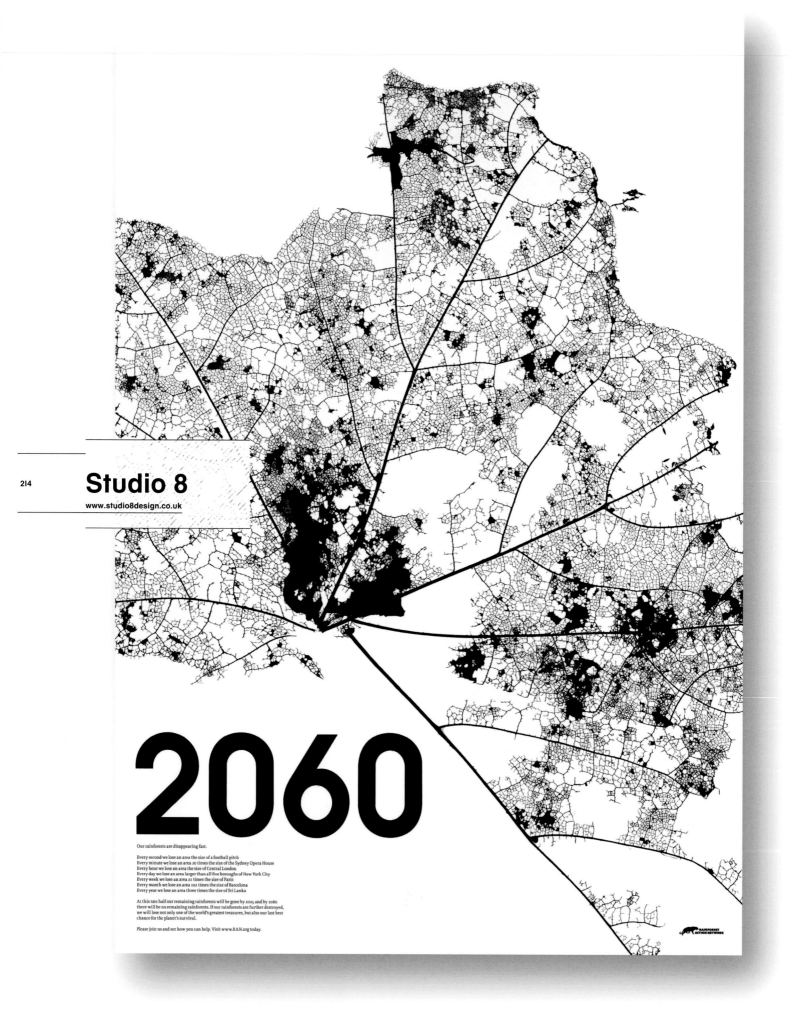

Studio 8
www.studio8design.co.uk

2060

Our rainforests are disappearing fast.

Every second we lose an area the size of a football pitch
Every minute we lose an area 20 times the size of the Sydney Opera House
Every hour we lose an area the size of Central London
Every day we lose an area larger than all five boroughs of New York City
Every week we lose an area 21 times the size of Paris
Every month we lose an area 102 times the size of Barcelona
Every year we lose an area three times the size of Sri Lanka

At this rate half our remaining rainforests will be gone by 2025 and by 2060
there will be no remaining rainforests. If our rainforests are further destroyed,
we will lose not only one of the world's greatest treasures, but also our last best
chance for the planet's survival.

Please join us and see how you can help. Visit www.R.A.N.org today.

AT THIS RATE | BOOK FOR ENVIRONMENTAL CHARITY RAN

How did you start?

Matt and I met at Frost design in 2002, where we were Creative Directors of the London studio, between 2003-5. We then freelanced independently for a number of clients, sharing a workspace alongside other designers in Hoxton. Amongst other things Matt was re-designing the Royal Academy's magazine and I was working with the Serpentine Gallery. We started Studio8 at the end of 2005. Matt heard of a studio space becoming free in Clerkenwell. We were both busy juggling a number of clients, and so joining forces to start the studio seemed like a natural progression.

Who are your main clients, and what type of work do you mainly do?

We are predominantly a print based design company and are probably known mostly for our editorial work – we work on a number of magazines, ranging from quarterly and bi-annual, to B to B magazines, where we are re-designing a magazine, and then handing over templates to an in-house design team. We also have a lot of clients in the cultural and charity sectors (The Association of Black Photographers; MAP Magazine; Laurence King Publishing; Chris Boot Publishing; The V&A; Headliners; The Rainforest Action Network; The Sorrell Foundation; The Circus Space; Plastique Magazine etc). However, for those clients we produce quite a diverse range of work across multiple disciplines including editorial, exhibition, signage, cor-porate literature, websites, and brand identity systems.

What time do you usually get to work? What time do you leave?

Officially, we start at 9.30. Often we're in earlier than that. Officially, we finish at 6.30. Occasionally, that happens.

Do you have a favourite place where you often meet up after work?

The 3 Kings in Clerkenwell Green. A much loved pub.

How would you say the design landscape has changed in the last 10 years?

There seems to be lots more small studios of 3 or 4 people doing great stuff and working with really interesting clients. The small studios seem to be competing more with much bigger, more established agencies and working with clients that previously might not have been brave enough to go with the small studio.

What would you say is the most distinctive characteristic of the visual arts in the UK?

Good ideas?

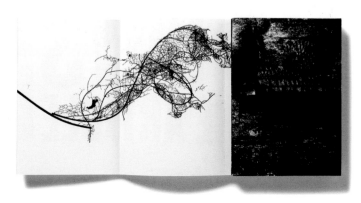

IT'S WHAT YOUR RIGHT ARM'S FOR

WE DO IT YOUR WAY

WE KEEP YOUR PROMISES

HEAD FOR THE BORDER

ONE LEG AT A TIME

WE'RE NUMBER TWO. WE TRY HARDER

WOT A LOT I GOT

FINGER-LICKIN' GOOD

WHILE IN EUROPE, PICK UP AN UGLY EUROPEAN

A LITTLE DAB'LL DO YA

CLEANS ROUND THE BEND

GEE, I WISH I HAD A NICKEL

JUST IMAGINE

LIVE TODAY. TOMORROW WILL COST MORE

ONLY 1 OUT OF 25 MEN IS COLOR BLIND. THE OTHER 24 JUST DRESS THAT WAY

HALITOSIS!

MAKE YOURSELF HEARD

TASTE AS GOOD AS IT SMELLS

WE SELL MORE CARS THAN FORD, CHRYSLER, CHEVROLET, AND BUICK COMBINED

LIMITED EDITION OF UNLIMITED IDEAS

PURE GENIUS

IT IS. ARE YOU?

SOFT, STRONG AND VERY LONG

PREPARE TO WANT ONE

IT'S SO BIG, YOU'VE GOTTA GRIN TO GET IT IN

THINK DIFFERENT

HELLO BOYS

BLOW SOME MY WAY

THE GENUINE ARTICLE

COME TO WHERE THE FLAVOR IS

EST
TWO

AN INTERVIEW WITH
FERNANDO GUTIÉRREZ

THE GREAT-
EST
THINGS
COME FROM
PEOPLE
TALKING

U
N
I
V
E
R
S
E
L
Y

I
S
E
V
E
R
Y
T
H
I
N
G

V
A
T
G

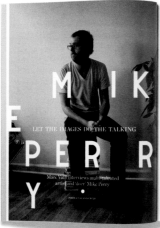

MIKE PERRY

LET THE IMAGES DO THE TALKING

Marc Valli interviews multi-talented
artist and doer Mike Perry

Brooklyn-based artist Mike Perry is just one of those people. He seems to be able to do so much work and cover so much ground that, in comparison, one cannot help asking oneself questions about one's own inactivity. It's like being in a vehicle going at moderate speed, and then being overtaken by a very fast one, and thinking, 'Have I stopped? Why am I not moving?'

Painter, illustrator, graphic artist, type-designer, art director, author, curator,.. Mike Perry won't be squeezed into a box. He shows with galleries. He works with big brands. He does catalogues for fashion labels, editorials for magazines, and ads for software and mobile phone companies. He does album covers. He creates his own products: t-shirts, adhesive tape with patterns, a Mike Perry snowboard for Salomon, a Mike Perry Iron-On kit for Chronicle Gifts, Mike Perry cushions, mugs, plates, and even a Mike Perry bandage strips box for Urban Outfitters. His books, Hand Job and Over & Over, both published by Princeton Architectural Press, have sold so well they have been reprinted more than once. He has started his own magazine, Untitled. He has even turned his hand to poetry.... And, amid all this, he finds time to reply to my emails – on the same day, as it happens. How does he do it?

PURE
TRUTH
VOID
NOW

PURE

UNIT EDITIONS

CASE STUDY NUMBER 1
HOW TO START A PUBLISHING COMPANY

Marc Valli talks to
Adrian Shaughnessy & Tony Brook (Spin)
about their ambitious new venture:
Unit Editions

ps.∂ arquitetura + design

CITIES

Creative City Guide

DESTINATION : SÃO PAULO

CITY GUIDE : SÃO PAULO

SAMPA

THINGS TO DO IN SÃO PAULO
WHEN YOU ARE NOT DEAD

by Marc Valli

SOMEW–
HERE
ELSE

ART   AND
DESIGN
PETER   AND
              SAVILLE

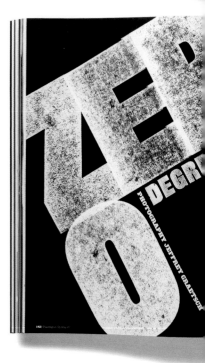

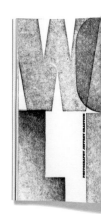

CONTRIBUTORS

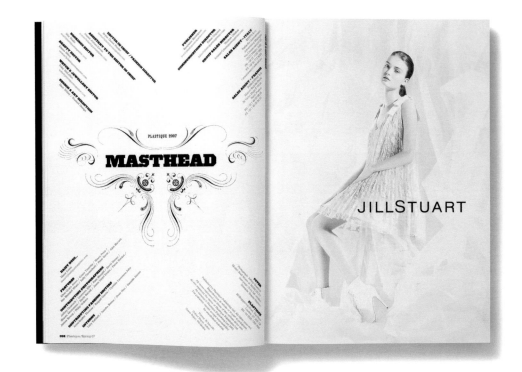

MASTHEAD

PLASTIQUE 2007

JILLSTUART

METAL LIC MASSI VE

PHOTOGRAPHY RAM SHERGILL

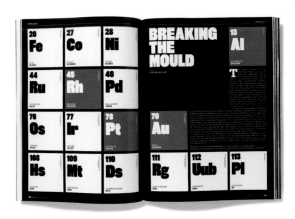

26 Fe	27 Co	28 Ni	**BREAKING THE MOULD**	13 Al
44 Ru	45 Rh	46 Pd		
76 Os	77 Ir	78 Pt	70 Au	
108 Hs	109 Mt	110 Ds	111 Rg	112 Uub	113 Pl

PHOTOGRAPHY MARI SARAI

NITE NITE

little yellow jacket
productions:
Only LYJ provides a
security camera, back
& laptop as standard,
on every job.

BESP OKE: BEFO

RE.... DURI NG..... & AI

FRANKLYN
RODGERS
THE PHILOSOPHY
OF STRANGERS

223

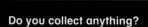

LOVE IXtra FOR BBC RADIO IXtra
RADIO STATION RELAUNCH CAMPAIGN
PRESS ADS. POSTERS. FLYERS.
BUS SHELTERS. ONLINE
2008

Studio Output

www.studio-output.com

How did you start?

Dan Moore and Rob Coke were working together as the senior design team at another Nottingham agency. Along with a client, Ian Hambleton, we decided that the time was right to do our own thing. We put together a business plan, borrowed some money from the bank and put some of our own savings into the pot. That was enough to buy some kit, rent a space and keep us paid for about three months in case we didn't get any work in. In the end were able to pay back our loan within about six months.

Who are your main clients, and what type of work do you mainly do?

Our key clients are BBC Radio I, Ministry of Sound, BBC IXtra (the BBC's digital black music station), Your Game, which is a sports' inclusion project run by BBC Sport, a high street fashion retailer called USC, a chain of restaurant/bars called Bluu and Sony PlayStation. We're currently concentrating design-led event campaigns, branding and interior graphic projects for bars/restaurants and various marketing materials for high street chains and bars.

Where is your studio based, and why?

We've got two studios: the first is in the Lace Market, in Nottingham. This was our only studio for five years. This was simply because we all lived here! Eventually we came around to the idea that it would be helpful for us to have a presence in London, so we opened a smaller studio in Clerkenwell, London, in June 2007. It's a great location because we've got some clients not far away and can also get to the West End quickly to see our clients at the BBC.

Do you collect anything?

I'm tempted to say we collect awards, but that's about as true as it is funny! We collect everything from books, magazines, records, Super-8 films, Modernist furniture, toys and packaging to ticket stubs, tax discs, pebbles, leaves and tree bark. Like a lot of places, we're gradually getting over-run by books and we try to encourage quite an eclectic mix in that department. Our walls are pretty clear other than some frames with images we've made, odds & ends from jobs which haven't happened and a large canvas of a world map that we created for a job a few years back. It gives the studio a feeling for world domination, like a James Bond villain's base.

Do you have a favourite place where you meet up after work?

Because people are often away, or travelling home, this doesn't always happen. Partly to make sure it does, we've been running a monthly meet-up called 'Glug' at the Commercial Tavern in London. It's a good chance for everyone to get together outside work, there are friends from other fields plus a few clients. We're just about to start Glug in Nottingham too, which is threatening to be bigger and better!

What about influences? Inspiration?

Influences, in no particular order: Herb Lubalin, Reid Miles, Ed Benguiat, Alan Fletcher, Frank Stella, James Rosenquist, 1960s art, textile patterns, Ken Garland, 1930s tube posters. Inspiration, in no particular order: music, current affairs, galleries, the walk home, our peers, secondhand shops, film, alcohol, the wonder of the universe, old gig posters, wartime posters, architecture, furniture, friends, travel.

How would you say the design landscape has changed in the last 10 years?

There's been a shift towards the designer as author and self-publicist, largely because of the prevalence of design blogs. This is a mixed blessing, because although you find more designers who are very self-motivated and aware, you also notice that people are looking at more and more current design, and everything starts to move in ever-decreasing circles. So a kind of international style has developed, which is all based on surface style rather than brief-driven problem solving. The best designers, as ever, are the ones who are just doing their own thing regardless.

What would you say is the most distinctive characteristic of the visual arts in the UK?

I think there needs to be a certain visual wit to it. That, and we like to think that we're responsible for everything, and constantly apologise for it. Sorry.

225

PUNK WOK FOR CONCEPT WORK
ART DIRECTION FOR SUSHI
RESTAURANT (CONCEPT IMAGES)
2008

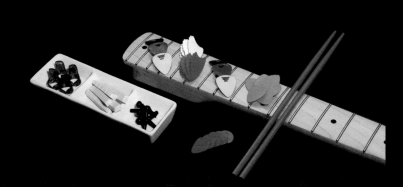

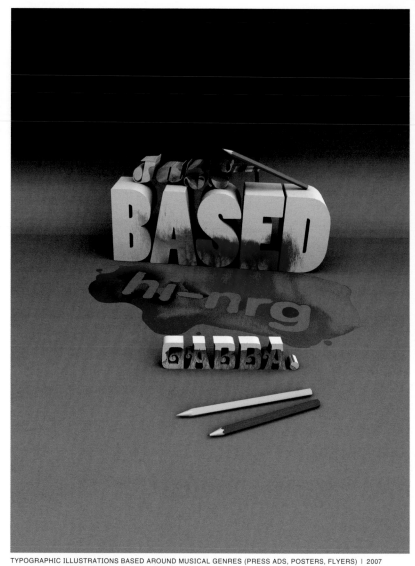

SATURDAY SESSIONS 'GENRES' | MINISTRY OF SOUND

TYPOGRAPHIC ILLUSTRATIONS BASED AROUND MUSICAL GENRES (PRESS ADS, POSTERS, FLYERS) | 2007

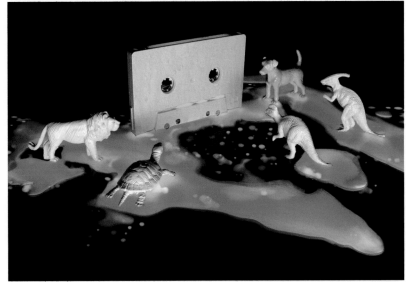

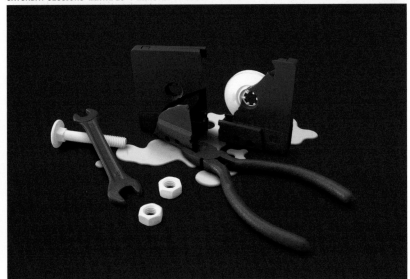

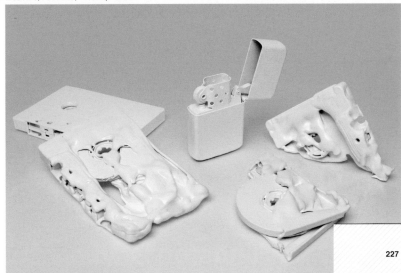

227

Tom Hingston Studio

www.hingston.net

**ARTWORK FOR SOLANGE
AZAGURY-PARTRIDGE WEBSITE**
A SERIES OF DETAILS TAKEN
FROM ANIMATIONS TOM
HINGSTON STUDIO CREATED
IN THEIR REDESIGN OF
THE NEW SOLANGE WEBSITE.

How did you start?

The studio was founded in 1997. Prior to that I had a full time job working for Neville Brody – around that time I also spent my evenings and weekends designing flyers for the Blue Note club in London's Hoxton Square. As the club blossomed, the workload increased and what started off as two maybe three flyers a week became ten or fifteen different bits of artwork, and slowly, it was becoming a full time job in itself. Something had to give – either the freelance, or my job – so I took the decision to set up on my own.

What type of work do you mainly do?

We are a multi–disciplinary studio working across a broad range of fields spanning music, fashion, film, motion graphics, advertising and branding. So our clients consist of musicians, film directors and fashion designers to brands such as Christian Dior, Lancôme or Nokia.

Where is your studio based?

We're based in Soho, London. It's fantastic being based here, but it was never a conscious decision on my part. I was initially offered a desk space by a friend of mine, who ran a record label over in Brewer Street. That was 11 years ago and we occupy two floors of this building now. The studio is comprised of five members - four designers and our studio manager.

Do you have a place where you meet up after work?

The Coffee House pub in Soho, one of the last decent pubs left in the area.

Do you collect anything?

I'm an avid collector of design and photography books, both contemporary and vintage. We have a big library here so the shelves are predominantly stacked high with books.

How would you say the design landscape has changed in the last 10 years?

The traditional model, or infrastructure of a design studio has changed enormously in recent times. Ten years ago design companies were mainly comprised of 6-8 people upwards. Due to the changes we've witnessed in technology it has empowered the individual. There are a lot more smaller design studios now consisting of just one or two people that have splintered away from bigger companies. The commissions they win and the work they're producing holds no bounds and can be anything from print, web or moving image. Because of the advances in the way we use technology, you no longer need 8 or 10 people to take on these kinds of projects as a design studio. - I think that's really exciting.

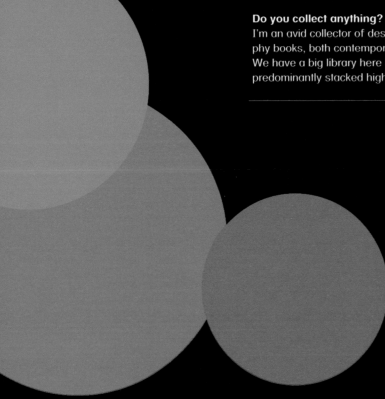

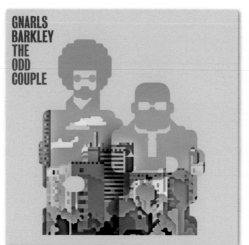

MASSIVE ATTACK "HELIGOLAND" | ALBUM | VIRGIN | 2010
ART DIRECTION AND DESIGN: TOM HINGSTON STUDIO
COVER ART: ROBERT DEL NAJA

NICK CAVE & AND THE BAD SEEDS "DIG, LAZARUS, DIG!!!"
MUTE | 2008

GNARLS BARKLEY "THE ODD COUPLE" | ALBUM | ATLANTIC | 2008

GNARLS BARKLEY "GOING ON" | SINGLE | ATLANTIC | 2008

GNARLS BARKLEY "GOING ON" – ALTERNATIVE COVER

GNARLS BARKLEY "RUN" | SINGLE | ATLANTIC | 2008

ZOOT WOMAN "ZOOT WOMAN" | ALBUM | WALL OF SOUND | 2003

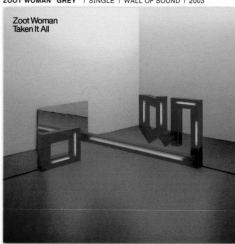

ZOOT WOMAN "GREY" | SINGLE | WALL OF SOUND | 2003

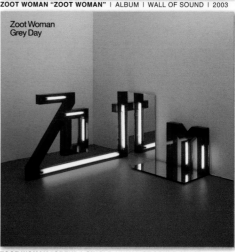

ZOOT WOMAN "TAKEN IT ALL" | SINGLE | WALL OF SOUND | 2003

ZOOT WOMAN "GEM" | SINGLE | WALL OF SOUND | 2003

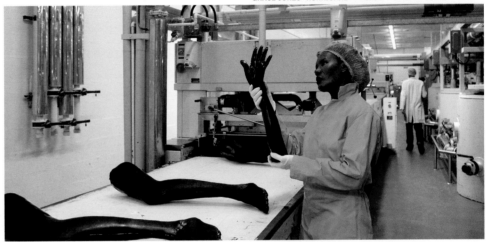

EDITORS "AN END HAS A START" | ALBUM | KITCHENWARE | 2007

GRACE JONES "HURRICANE" | ALBUM | WALL OF SOUND | 2008

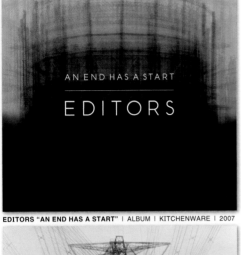

EDITORS "THE RACING RATS" | SINGLE | KITCHENWARE | 2007

EDITORS "AN END HAS A START" | SINGLE | KITCHENWARE | 2007

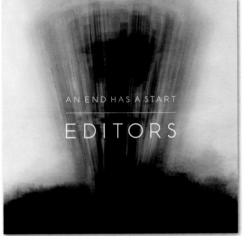

ARTWORK FOR GRACE JONES "HURRICANE"
ART DIRECTION AND DESIGN: TOM HINGSTON STUDIO
PHOTOGRAPHY: JONATHAN DE VILLIERS

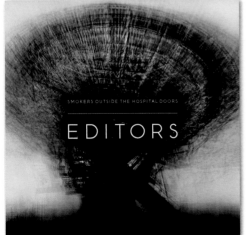

EDITORS "SMOKERS OUTSIDE THE HOSPITAL DOORS"
SINGLE | KITCHENWARE | 2007

GRACE JONES "HURRICANE" | VINYL | 2008

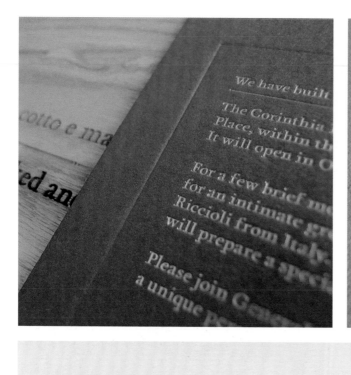

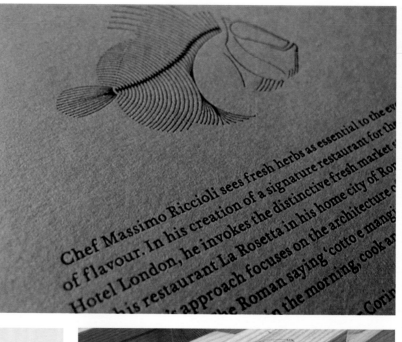

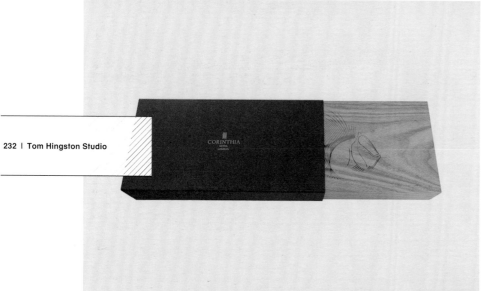

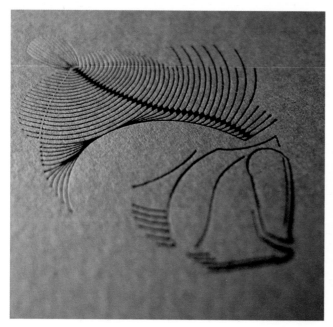

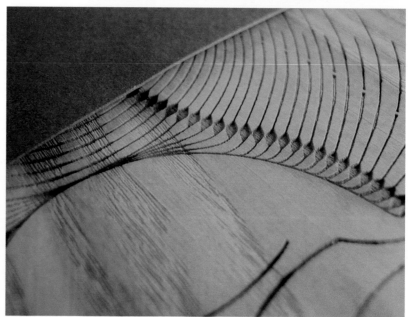

CORINTHIA | IDENTITY, INVITATION AND PROMOTIONAL MATERIAL
FOR LONDON BASED POP-UP RESTAURANT.

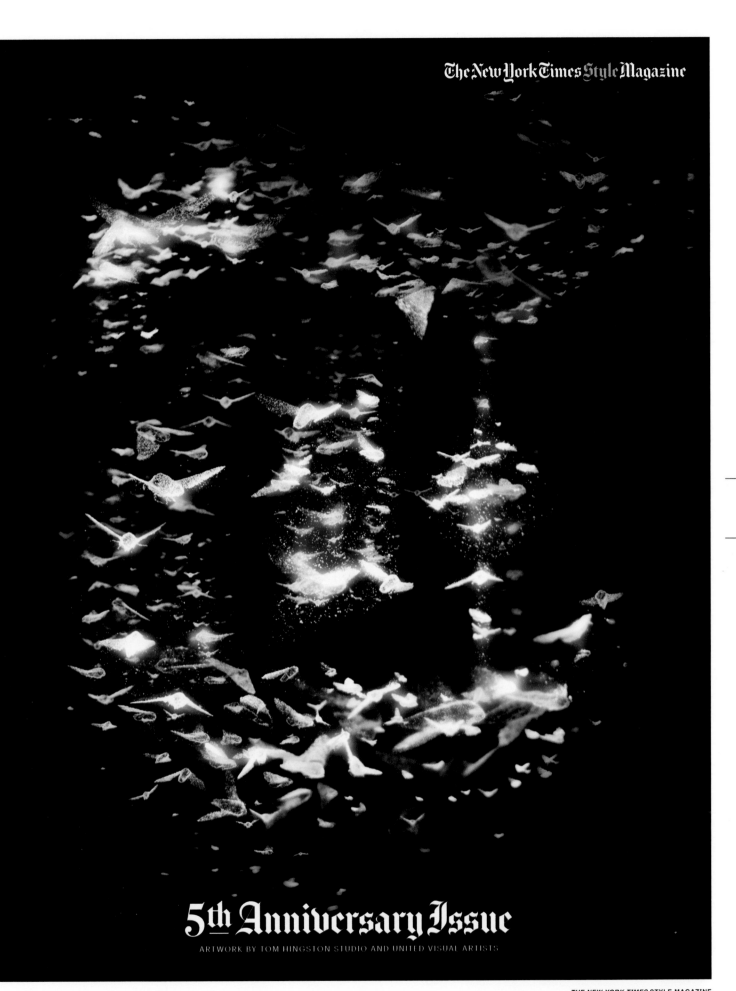

5th Anniversary Issue

ARTWORK BY TOM HINGSTON STUDIO AND UNITED VISUAL ARTISTS

THE NEW YORK TIMES STYLE MAGAZINE
TO CELEBRATE THE 5TH ANNIVERSARY ISSUE 5 ARTISTS WERE COMMISSIONED
TO INTERPRET THE ICONIC T FOR THE COVER OF NEW YORK TIMES FOR
THEIR MAGAZINE T. THE UVA & TOM HINGSTON T COLLABORATION ALSO EXTENDS
TO AN ACCOMPANYING FILM ON-LINE, FEATURING MUSIC BY MIRA CALIX.

Tomato
www.tomato.co.uk

How did Tomato start?
Tomato was born out of the collapse of the late eighties, and a frustration at the way the design/advertising industry was restricting the process of making work. Creativity through exploration was at the root of the desire to make change.

What is the background of the founders
Painter, film-maker, designer, musician, writer.

What type of work do you mainly do?
Our recent projects have included: commissions from industry and government to produce large scale public installations, design and art-direction for publishing, web design, film and video commissions for TV and music. title sequences and motion graphics, some branding and re-branding.

How many partners do you now have?
Eight.

Where is your studio based?
Clerkenwell, London. Nice space—inside and outside.

How do you get to work?
Bike. Train. Vespa. Tube. Taxi.

Do you have a favourite place where you often meet up after work?
Meson Los Barrilles, Goswell Road, Clerkenwell.

How would you describe your studio?
A simple living-room, big, with a comfy sofa and turntables.

How many of you work there?
Up to six at any one time.

What kind of music gets played in the studio?
It varies from rave to musique concrete...
1. only have eyes for you/lester bowies brass fantasy
2. no wow/the kills
3. take your soul/the sahara all stars of jos
4. silver apples of the moon/morton subotnick
5. i'm in love with a german film star/ the passions
6. the end/john carpenter
7. carolina drama/the raconteurs
8. sex-o-matic/edu k
9. just your fool/little walter
10. night drive/model 500

Where or what do you turn to for inspiration?
Cities, people and each other.

How would you say the design landscape has changed in the last 10 years?
A huge democratization across the creative fields through the advent and distribution of technology. this has lead to individuals working across all media platforms... for better... or worse.

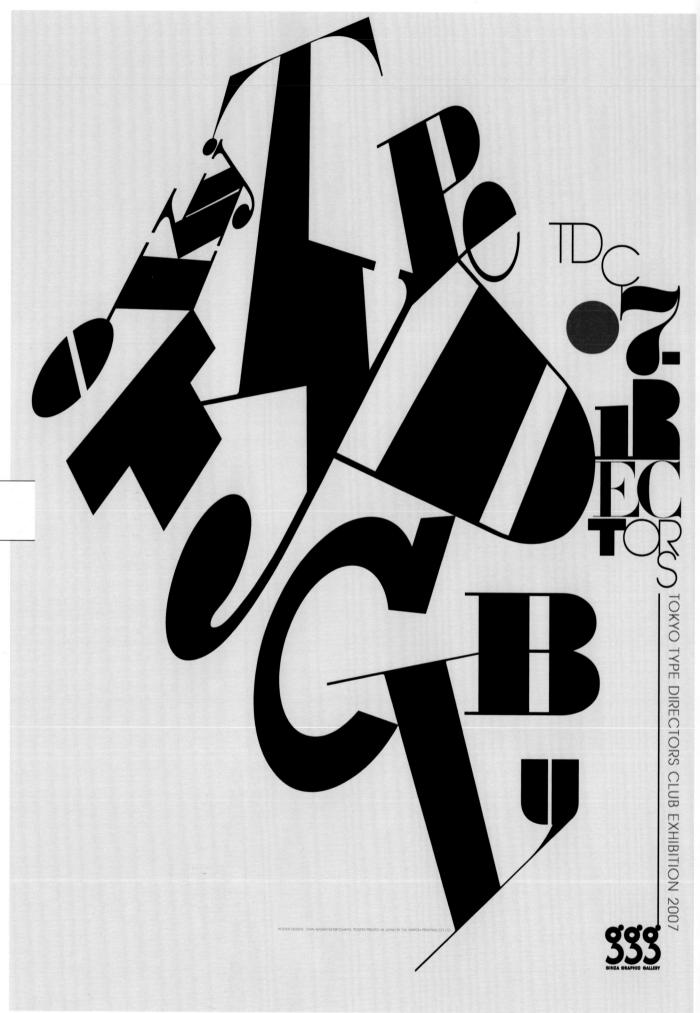

UNDERWORLD 'PLAYPIG' | 12 INCH SLEEVE | 2007

QI (QUANTA) TYPOGRAPHIC DESIGN | 2006

UNDERWORLD 'BOY BOY BOY' | 12 INCH SLEEVE | 2007

UNDERWORLD 'CROCODILE' | 12 INCH SLEEVE | 2007

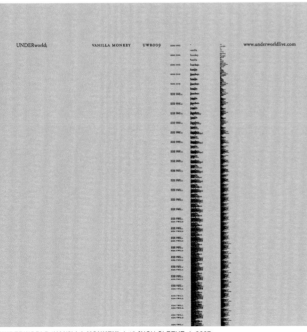

UNDERWORLD 'VANILLA MONKEY' | 12 INCH SLEEVE | 2007

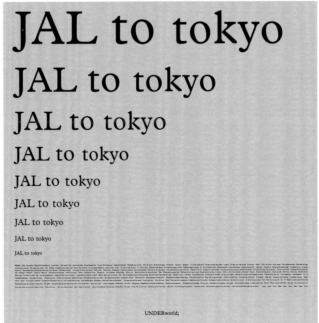

UNDERWORLD 'JAL TO TOKYO' | 12 INCH SLEEVE | 2007

NOUVELLE VAGUE "3" | VINYL/CD SLEEVE | 2009

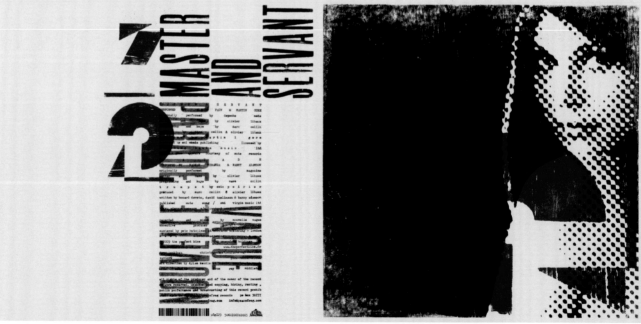

NOUVELLE VAGUE "MASTER AND SERVANT" | VINYL 7 INCH SINGLE | 2009

NOUVELLE VAGUE "DEBUT ALBUM" | VINYL/CD SLEEVE | 2004

NOUVELLE VAGUE "JUST CAN'T GET ENOUGH" | VINYL 10 INCH SLEEVE | 2004

NOUVELLE VAGUE "GUNS OF BRIXTON" | VINYL 10 INCH SLEEVE | 2004

NOUVELLE VAGUE "BANDE Á PART" | VINYL/CD SLEEVE | 2006

NOUVELLE VAGUE "BANDE Á PART" – SAMPLER | VINYL/CD SLEEVE | 2006

NOUVELLE VAGUE "EVER FALLEN IN LOVE" | VINYL/CD SINGLE SLEEVE | 2006

Universal Everything
www.universaleverything.com

AUDI TT VIRAL VIDEO
MATT PYKE & KARSTEN SCHMIDT

How did you start?
I was drawing from the day i picked up a pencil. My brother, a musician, asked me to design his record sleeves. The Designers Republic saw them and hired me. A friend at the Apple product design team encouraged me to start Universal Everything.

What type of work do you mainly do?
We work with everything from pencils and stop motion, to film directors and generative design. We have worked with galleries including the V&A and MOMA, and clients from London 2012 Olympics, to Nokia and Audi

Where is your studio based?
Sheffield, with its proximity to peak district ensures we look beyond the regular sphere of influences

How do you get to work?
A 25 metre commute to the studio in the garden

What time do you usually get to work?
9am

What time do you leave?
5pm

How would you describe your studio?
It flits between super-minimal digital production-space, and paint-splattered, leaf-covered idea-space.

How many of you work there?
Between I and 4.

What's on the walls?
Our walls are covered in cork, pinned with 1000 ideas.

What kind of music gets played?
Vanity Fair by Mr Bungle, Make Me Believe In You by Patti Jo, What Up by Busta Rhymes, Delfonics Theme by The Delfonics, Sea Song by Robert Wyatt, Left Leg Out by Digital Mystix.

Do you collect anything?
Email addresses.

What would you say is the most distinctive characteristic of graphic and the visual arts in the UK?
Pushing beyond the zeitgeist with a respect for history.

Village Green Studio
www.villagegreenstudio.com

FABRIC SATURDAY
MONTHLY PROMOTIONAL POSTERS,
FOR SATURDAY NIGHT AT LONDON BASED NIGHTCLUB
FABRIC.

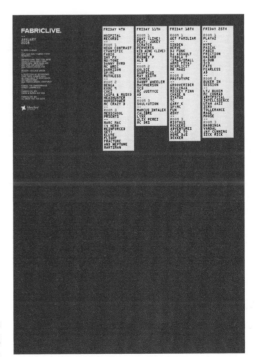

How did you start?

Seb was a founder of design agency Blue Source. Jonathon worked at Blue Source for a few years in the 1990's, before setting up his own studio, Love. Jonathon and Seb knew each other from working together in the past. After collaborating on a couple of projects they decided they had more fun with these than the day jobs. They both decided to close their own studio and start Village Green. That was in early 2007. The other people are Tom, Tom, Peter and Andrew

What type of work do you mainly do?

We've done our share of advertising and music design, but also branding and identity work. Also the ongoing poster series promoting Fabric in London and some smaller print design projects for nice people. We've a diverse range of clients including, bands, ad agencies, promoters, broadcasters, artists, fashion and textile designers and jewellers.

Where is your studio based?

A basement in EC1 in London. Because it's quite central, it's quite cheap and it's quite big. But there isn't enough light.

Do you have a place where you meet up after work?

When we can… The Wenlock Arms, Wenlock Street

How would you describe your studio?

We collect things, the furniture is a mix of collected mid 20th century furniture and bespoke designed pieces. There is more clutter than we want. We have a lot of books, so the library is the most thought out part.

Do you collect anything?

We collect books, furniture, old paintings. Peter builds and collects bikes, Jonathon is into vintage clothing. There is an old country gate mounted on the wall with a sunrise design.

245

FABRIC LIVE
MONTHLY PROMOTIONAL POSTERS,
FOR FRIDAY NIGHT AT LONDON BASED
NIGHTCLUB FABRIC.

246 | Village Green Studio

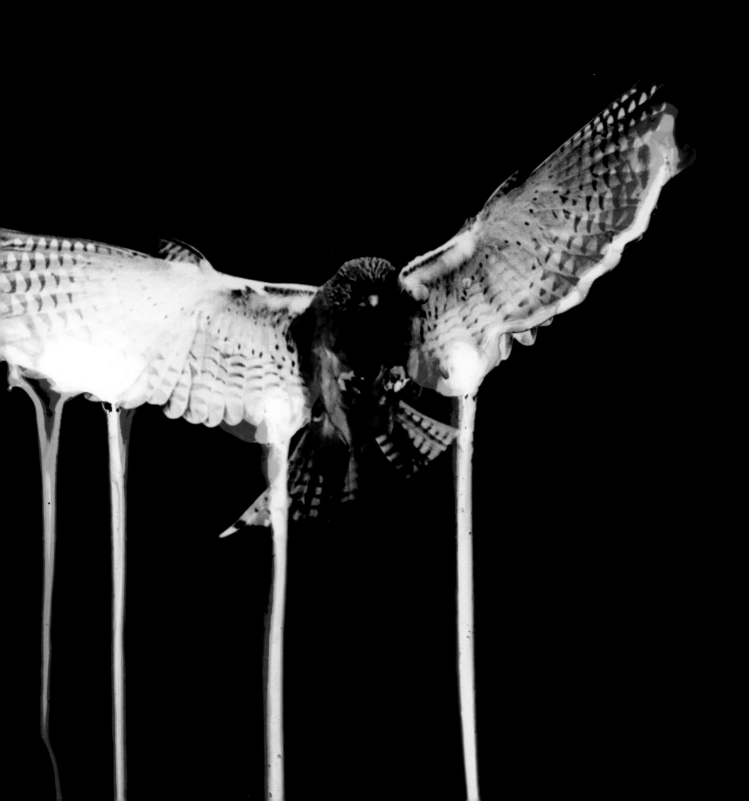

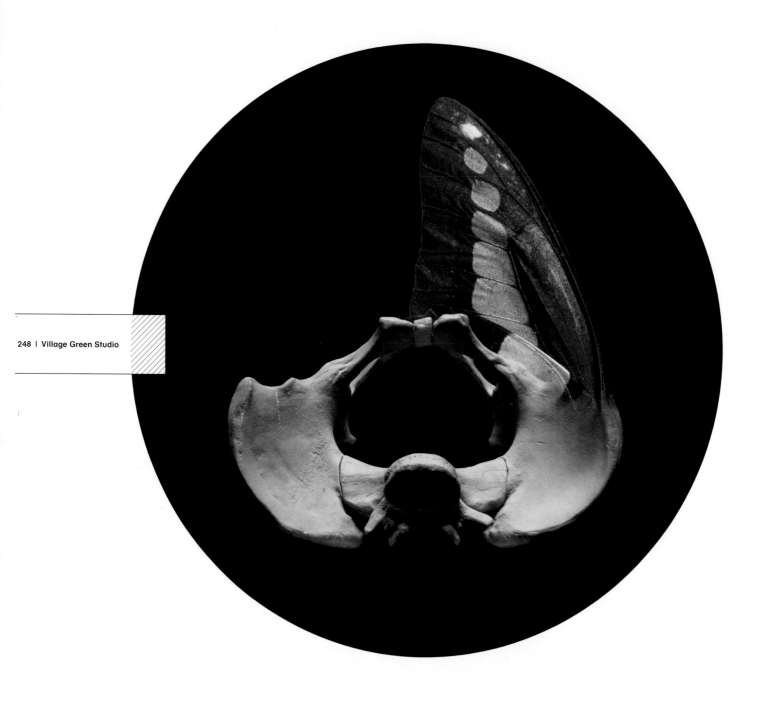

**IMAGES FOR FASHION EDITORIAL FOR
032C MAGAZINE (BERLIN).**
PHOTOGRAPHY BY DAVID HUGHES.

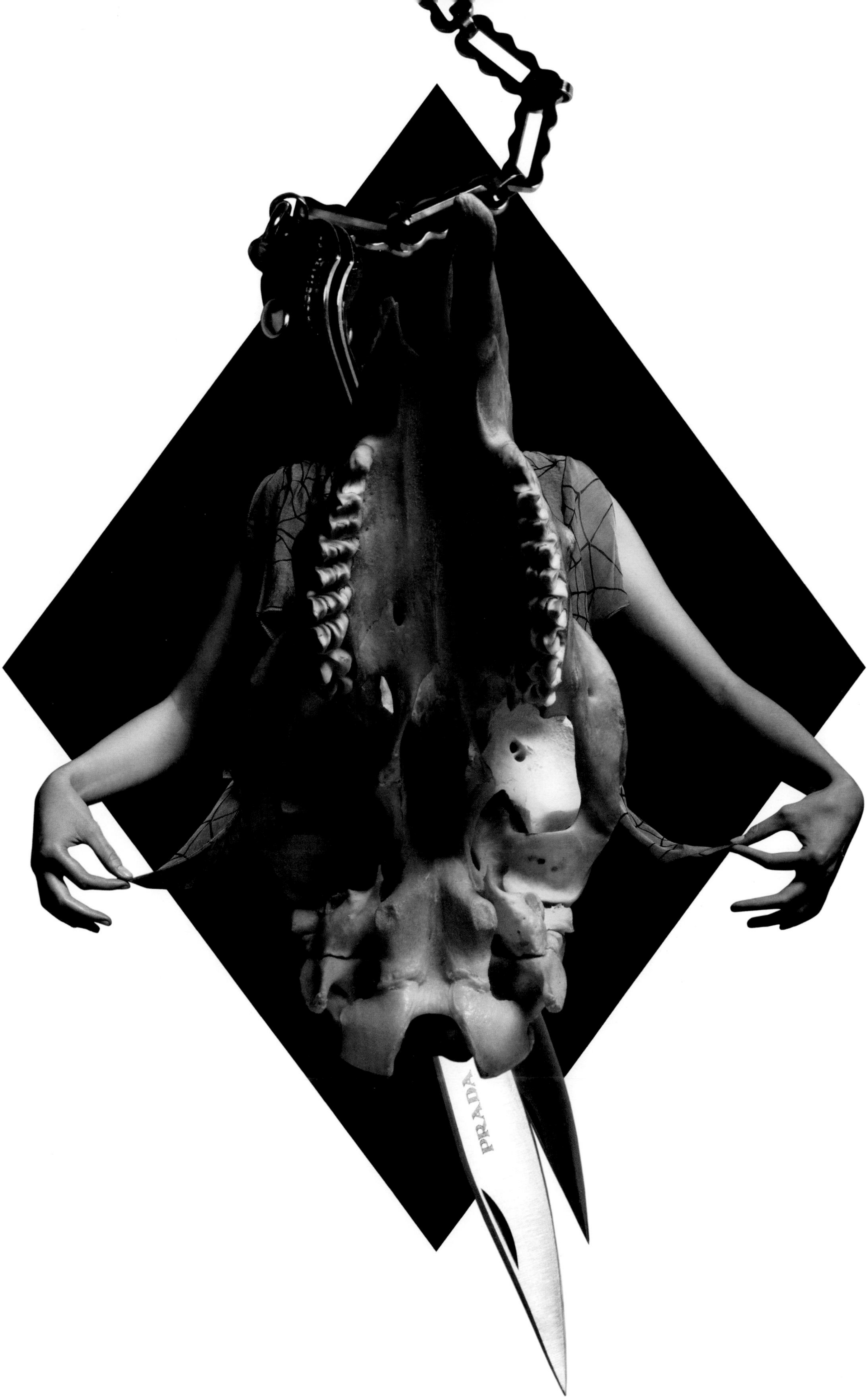
PRADA

MARK RONSON
ALBUM AND SINGLES CAMPAIGN
SONY BMG | 2007

THE WHIP   TRASH

1 RADIO EDIT
2 ORIGINAL
3 LETS GO TO WAR REMIX
4 CROOKERS REMIX
5 SOUTH CENTRAL REMIX

℗ & © Southern Fried Records 2008. The Whip are Bruce Carter, Danny Saville, Fiona Daniel and Nathan Sudders. Written by Bruce Carter and Danny Saville. Copyright Control. Produced by Jim Abbiss, Bruce Carter and Danny Saville. Additional production by Liam Howe. Recorded by Richard Wilkinson at Konk Studios and in 100's of places by Danny and Bruce. Mixed by Damian Taylor at Strongroom Studios. Assistant engineers Serge Krebbs, Ben Mason and Ian Dowling. Track 3 appears courtesy of Last Gang Records Inc. Track 4 remix and additional production by Crookers. Track 5 remix and production by Keith Camilleri and Robert Chetcuti for South Central. Design by Village Green. ECB141CDS. This single is taken from the album 'X Marks Destination' www.myspace.com/thewhipmanchester

252

Craig Ward words are pictures

www.wordsarepictures.co.uk

INK AND WATER DON'T MIX
FONTLAB | TYPOGRAPHY
EMBELLISHED WITH INK
AND WATER. I TRACED ELEMENTS
OF EACH LETTER USING A
FOUNTAIN PEN AND DRIPPED
WATER ON THEM FROM ABOVE.
2008

IT'S A BEAUTIFUL DECAY | FONTLAB
TYPE SAMPLE OF A PHOTOFONT I CREATED
USING DYING BLOSSOMS | 2008

How did you start?

I graduated in 2003 from a design and illustration course and quickly found work in a below-the-line advertising agency in Central London. Within a few months, I began to realise that this was not going to be enough for me creatively and so I started working on self initiated projects outside of work. Eventually I had a large enough body of work to warrant a website and it was through this that I received my first paid commission for *The New York Times.*

What type of work do you mainly do?

With a few exceptions my clients so far have been one-offs in the publishing, editorial and advertising fields. I'm generally brought in to create a bespoke type treatment for a headline, or an article, or cover in a variety of mediums from hand-drawn and letter-pressed to digitally created or 3D treatments. I don't have a style, rather an approach – working with type means I can have as many styles as there are typefaces and then as many treatments as I can come up with for each of them, I find that fact very exciting.

Do you collect anything?

Aside from my wooden type I try to keep my own clutter to a minimum, although every time I'm in Spain (my girlfriend has family out there), I seem to pick up locksmith stickers. In this town where her grandma lives every doorway is covered in hundreds of different ones, seems people in Spain lose their keys a lot. I also collect collectors; I have an excellent archive of other people's collections of things from fruit stickers, typographic onomatopoeias from the 1960's Batman TV series, film opening credits – pretty much anything that exists in vast quantities really. On my walls you'll find a mixture of reasonably large black and white photographs of cities my girlfriend and I have visited, a couple of screen prints and some old French illustrations that we picked up on the cheap in Paris. My shelves are literally heaving with design books, type sample books, type mixers, printing process books... Too many to mention but I don't want to move for a while.

Who/what are your main influences?

My main influences are designers like Alan Fletcher and Saul Bass – I can really subscribe to their symbolise and simplify maxim. And I like all my work, in some shape or form, to have a reward for the viewer too – some nice little touch that makes you smile when you get it. Conversely, I like to take inspiration from those younger than me. I know I've only been graduated for 5 years or so but good placement students come to the table with no concept of budgets, timings and plausibility – they're just bristling with ideas and that's a really important thing to try and keep hold of.

What would you say is the most distinctive characteristic of the visual arts in the UK?

Is diversity a characteristic? As a nation we don't have a style per sé, but it is unified by it's disparity – a book like this will showcase a hundred different ways of working and approaching a brief and I think that's really important.

ALL WORK AND NO PLAY | FONTLAB
TYPE SAMPLE OF A PHOTOFONT I CREATED
USING HAIR | 2008

WISH YOU WERE HERE | ELVIS COMMUNICATIONS, LONDON | AI SIZED PAPERCUT ILLUSTRATION FOR THE WALLS OF ELVIS' OFFICE | 2008

poems by
MOSTAFA
MAJIDI

A&P | ACCEPT AND PROCEED,
LONDON | TREATMENT / PHOTOGRAPHIC
SOLUTION TO AN OPEN BRIEF PUT
OUT BY A&P TO INTERPRET THEIR LOGO
2008

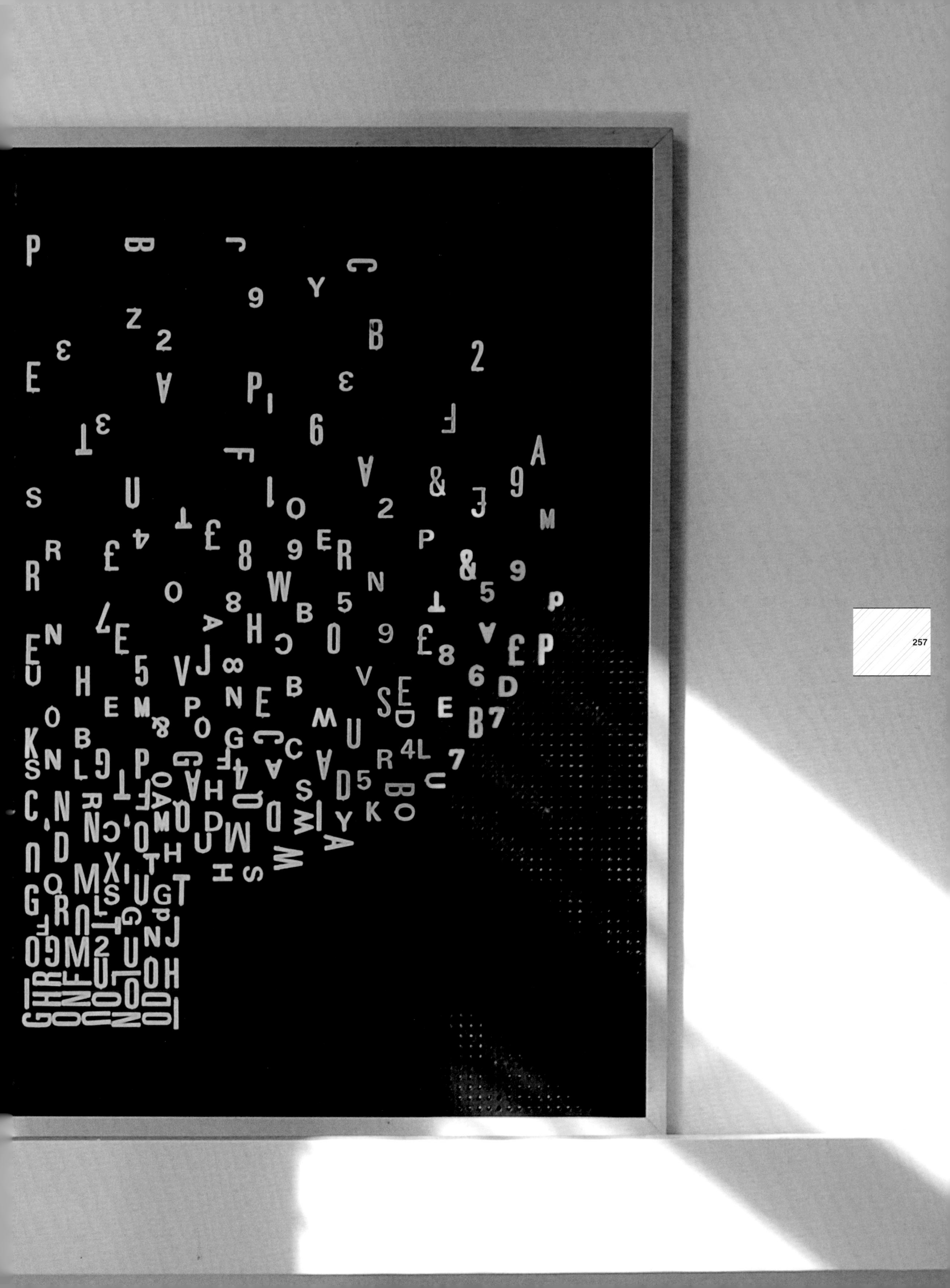

BADOOD
TYPOGR
GRAAPHY
IS IS
EVERYSI
BLWHERE

**GOOD TYPOGRAPHY IS INVISIBLE /
BAD TYPOGRAPHY IS EVERYWHERE /**

PRESENTING A SERIES OF WORKSHOPS FOR SECOND YEAR GRAPHIC DESIGN PATHWAY STUDENTS
LOOKING AT THE FUNDAMENTALS OF TYPOGRAPHY AND MOVABLE TYPE, INCLUDING LETTERPRESS
AND TYPESETTING. WORKSHOPS BEGIN IN APRIL AND WILL TAKE PLACE AT BUCKS NEW COLLEGE,
HIGH WYCOMBE. FOR MORE INFORMATION, SPEAK TO PAUL PLOWMAN OR REGISTER YOUR INTEREST
BY EMAILING INFO@WORDSAREPICTURES.CO.UK

bucks
new university

**GOOD TYPOGRAPHY IS INVISIBLE /
BAD TYPOGRAPHY IS EVERYWHERE**
BUCKS NEW UNIVERSITY, HIGH WYCOMBE
POSTER INTRODUCING A SHORT
COURSE I CONDUCTED AT MY FORMER
UNIVERSITY | 2008

LET'S GO GET LOST
SELF INITIATED 3D
REALISATION OF LYRICS BY
THE RED HOT
CHILI PEPPERS | 2009

why not associates

www.whynotassociates.com

CATALOGUE & INVITATION
FOR CHRIS LEVINE'S EXHIBITION
LIGHTNESS OF BEING

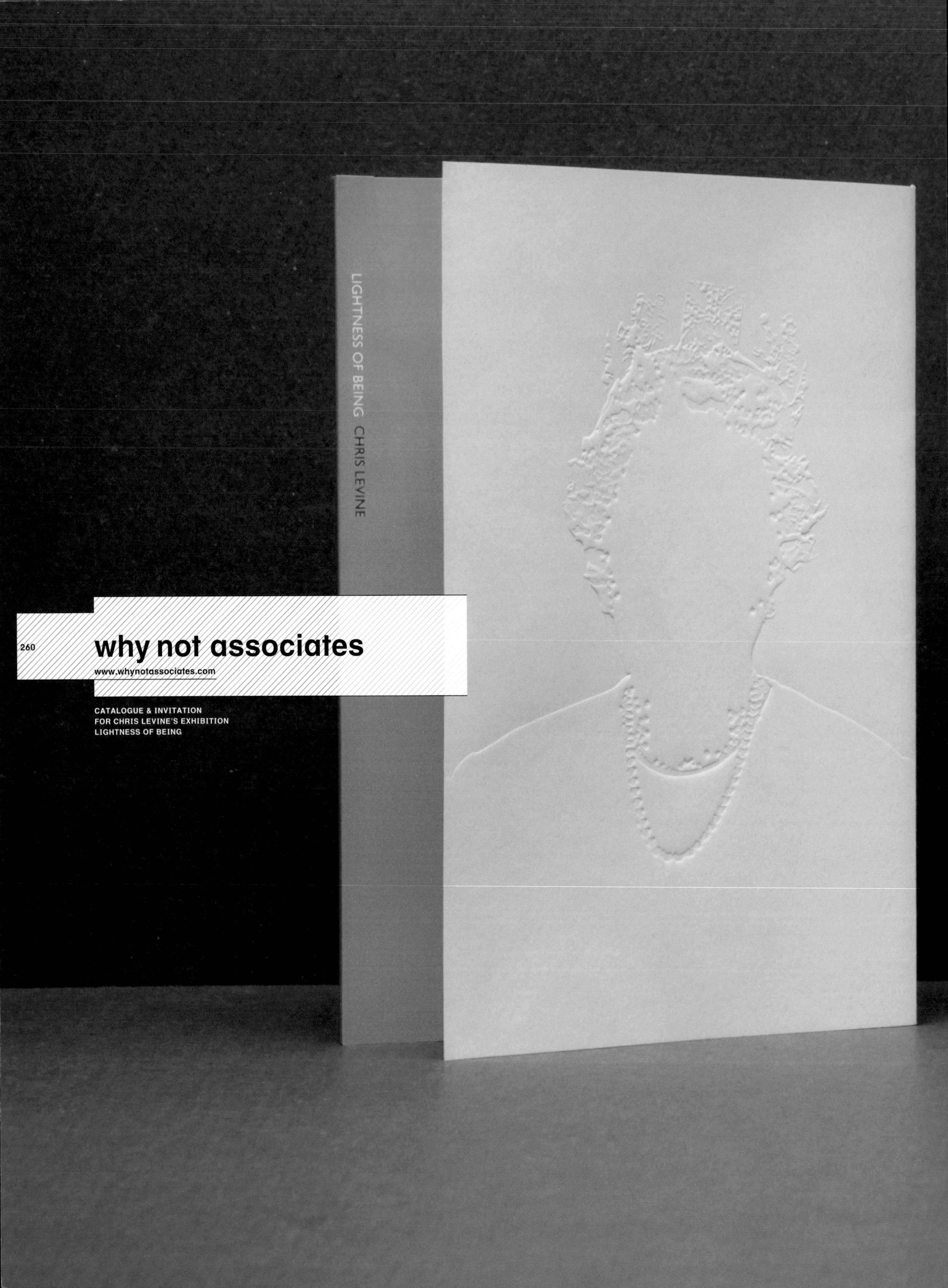

LIGHTNESS OF BEING   CHRIS LEVINE

How did you start?
Why not associates was formed late in 1987 by Andy Altmann, David Ellis and Howard Greenhalgh. Both David and I (Andy) had attended Saint Martins school of art in London. Howard had attended the London College of Printing. We were all at the Royal College of Art from 1985 to 1987. Howard was asked to design a magazine while at college and asked myself (Andy) and David to help. We started the first issue on the day we left college and it snowballed from there. Howard left why not associates several years ago and works as a highly successful commercials director.

Who are your clients?
Our clients are varied, as is the work we produce, from postage stamps to typographic pavements via directing television commercials and exhibition graphics. Clients include: the Royal Mail, Nike, BBC, the Tate Modern, the Royal Academy of Arts, London College of Fashion. There is no one type of work we specialise in.

Where are you based?
Old street, London. We were in Soho for our first 12 years, but moved to Old street as it was a cheaper area and we wanted more space. We're now 2 partners and 6 full time staff.

Where do you go for a drink?
There is a great pub around the corner called the Wenlock Arms.

What are your main influences?
Our favourite artists/designers are: Eric Gill, Ed Ruscha, Piet Zwart, Kurt Schwitters, Isamu Noguchi. I am inspired by everything.

How would you say the design landscape has changed in the last 10 years?
It used to be like the surface of the moon – now it's like a baby's bottom.

What would you say is the most distinctive characteristic of the visual arts in the UK?
Punk and pageantry.

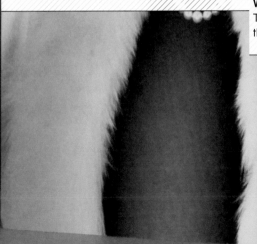

261

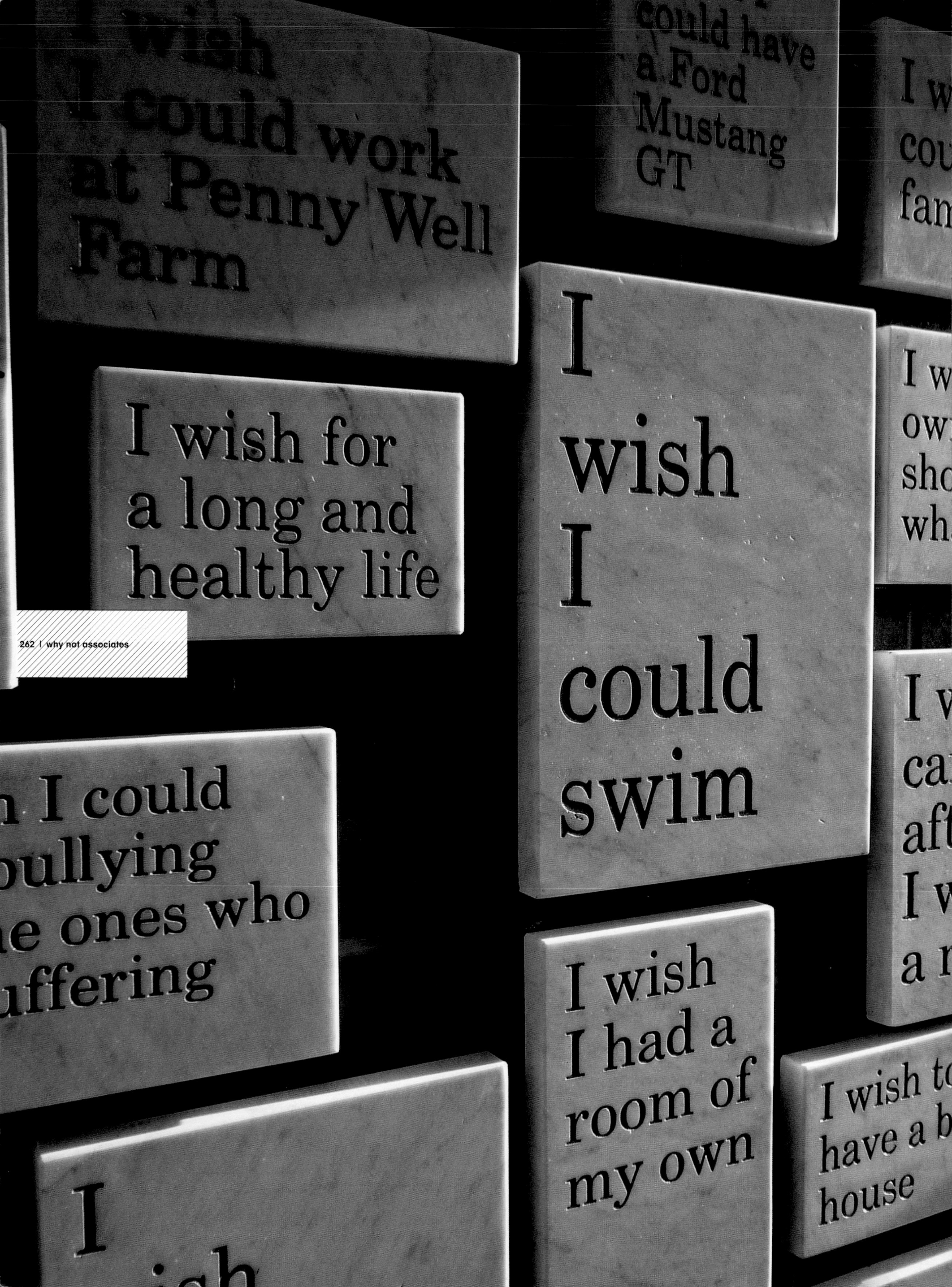

I wish
I could work
at Penny Well
Farm

could have
a Ford
Mustang
GT

I wish for
a long and
healthy life

I wish
I
could
swim

I could
bullying
e ones who
uffering

I wish
I had a
room of
my own

I wish to
have a b
house

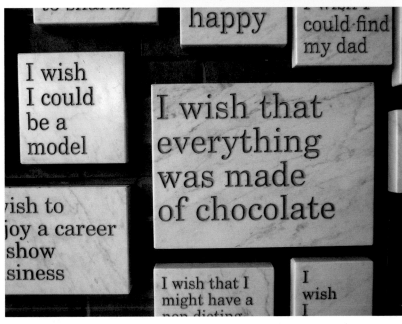

BRUNEL ACADEMY'S WALL OF WISHES | SCHOOL ENTRANCE

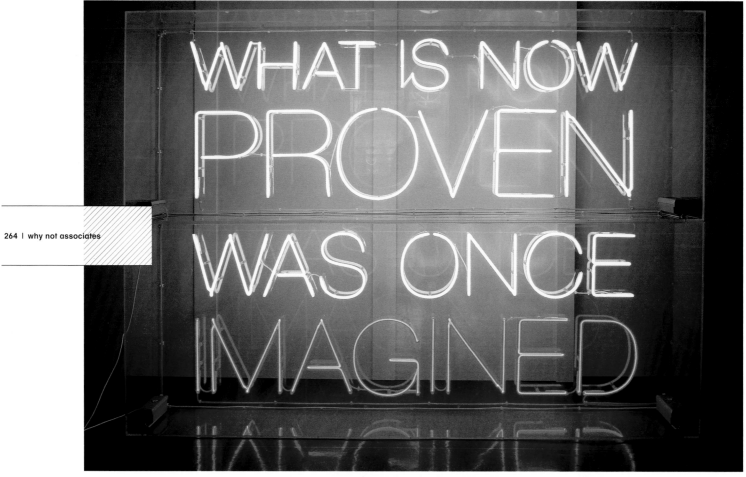

WHAT IS NOW PROVEN WAS ONCE IMAGINED | BRUNEL ACADEMY'S NEON LETTERING

265

JULIAN GERMAIN
*FOR EVERY MINUTE YOU ARE
ANGRY YOU LOSE SIXTY
SECONDS OF HAPPINESS*
PHOTOGRAPHY BOOK
PUBLISHED BY STEIDL MACK

William Hall
www.williamhall.co.uk

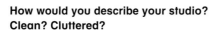

Where is your studio based?
Clerkenwell. It's central and a nice place to be.

How would you describe your studio? Clean? Cluttered?
Clean and uncluttered. We have a clear desk policy, and this extends to the digital desktop. Only documents that are currently in use are kept out. I think the way we operate in the office is important. I will never understand design companies who claim to consider every aspect of their clients' branding, and then you go to the kitchen and all the mugs are dirty and broken, and the bins are overflowing. We take special care with the rituals of daily working life – especially tea.

How many of you work there? What music do you play?
There's a lot of silence, and a lot of Radiohead, Bob Dylan, and Soulwax. We're currently working on videos for Hook & The Twin, so they get played a lot too.

Do you collect anything? What's on your walls?
I don't collect anything, unless you count books, but that really isn't about accumulation, and the ownership isn't important.
The walls are mostly bare, with a few items that change regularly. The wall is a something of a sketchbook for me. Currently on the wall are an A0 sheet of white Chromolux, an A0 running sheet from a book we've just finished, a postcard of Portrait of a Knight of Malta by Caravaggio, a postcard of The Interior of The Grote Kerk at Haarlem by Pieter Saenredam, an A3 image showing the extent of WW2 bombing in Rotherhithe, and an A4 sheet with a Robert Frost poem 'Stopping by Woods on a Snowy Evening'.

How did you start?
I studied at Central Saint Martins, graduating in 1997, and always had my own work, although initially I did freelance work for a few days a week with a series of companies including a five year period at the office of the minimalist architect, John Pawson. I set up formally in 2003. I work with a small team of people, complemented by a group of experienced freelancers.

Who are your main clients, and what type of work do you mainly do?
Our regular clients include Henry Moore Institute, Haunch of Venison, Fourth Estate, London College of Fashion, Tate, and the architect John Pawson. Most of our projects are books and small-scale identities, although we are increasingly working on art direction and websites.

Who/what are your main influences? Where do you draw inspiration from?
I suppose Mies van der Rohe, Dieter Rams, and Adolf Loos are influences. But really I turn to the brief for inspiration. We have a methodical and deliberative approach, which slightly negates the need for 'inspiration'.

What would you say is the most distinctive characteristic of the visual arts in the UK?
We are quite spoilt in the UK, when working in the arts with enlightened and interested clients, but there is a long way to go before big business really embraces the talents and skills of the best graphic designers. For example, I think we are set to be hugely underwhelmed by the London Olympics graphics over the next four years.

269

WE NOT I ARCHITECTS | IDENTITY & STATIONERY

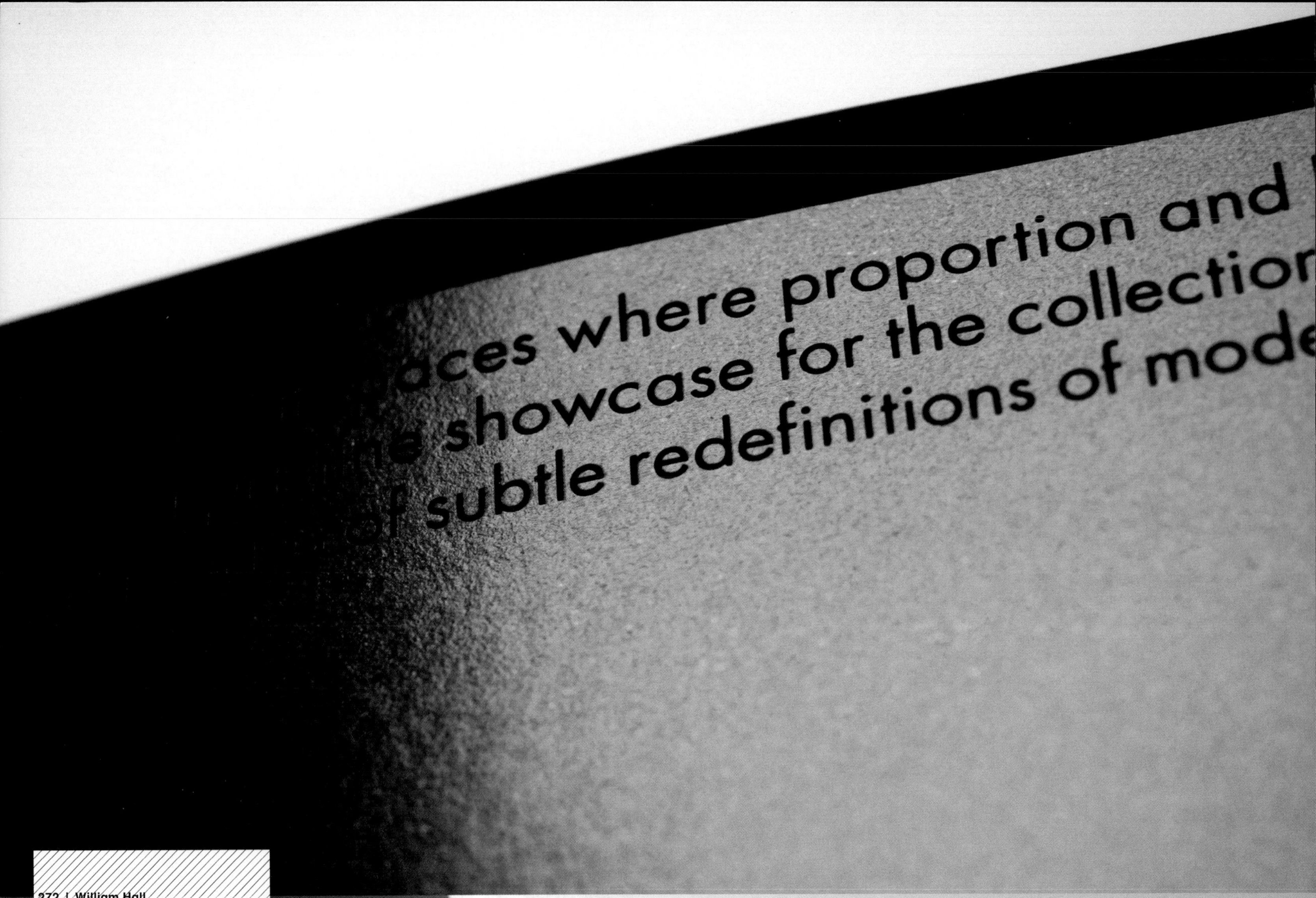

aces where proportion and
e showcase for the collection
f subtle redefinitions of mode

CALVIN KLEIN | CATALOGUE FOR NEW PARIS, AVENUE MONTAIGNE, SHOP

sensual spaces
a pristine showcase
eries of subtle

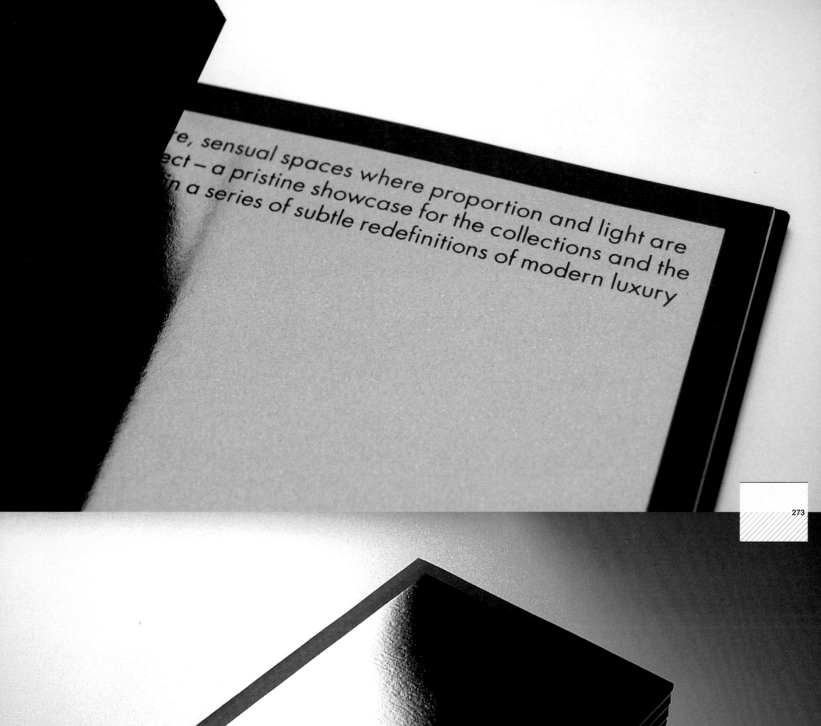

re, sensual spaces where proportion and light are
ect – a pristine showcase for the collections and the
n a series of subtle redefinitions of modern luxury

Winkreative
www.winkreative.com

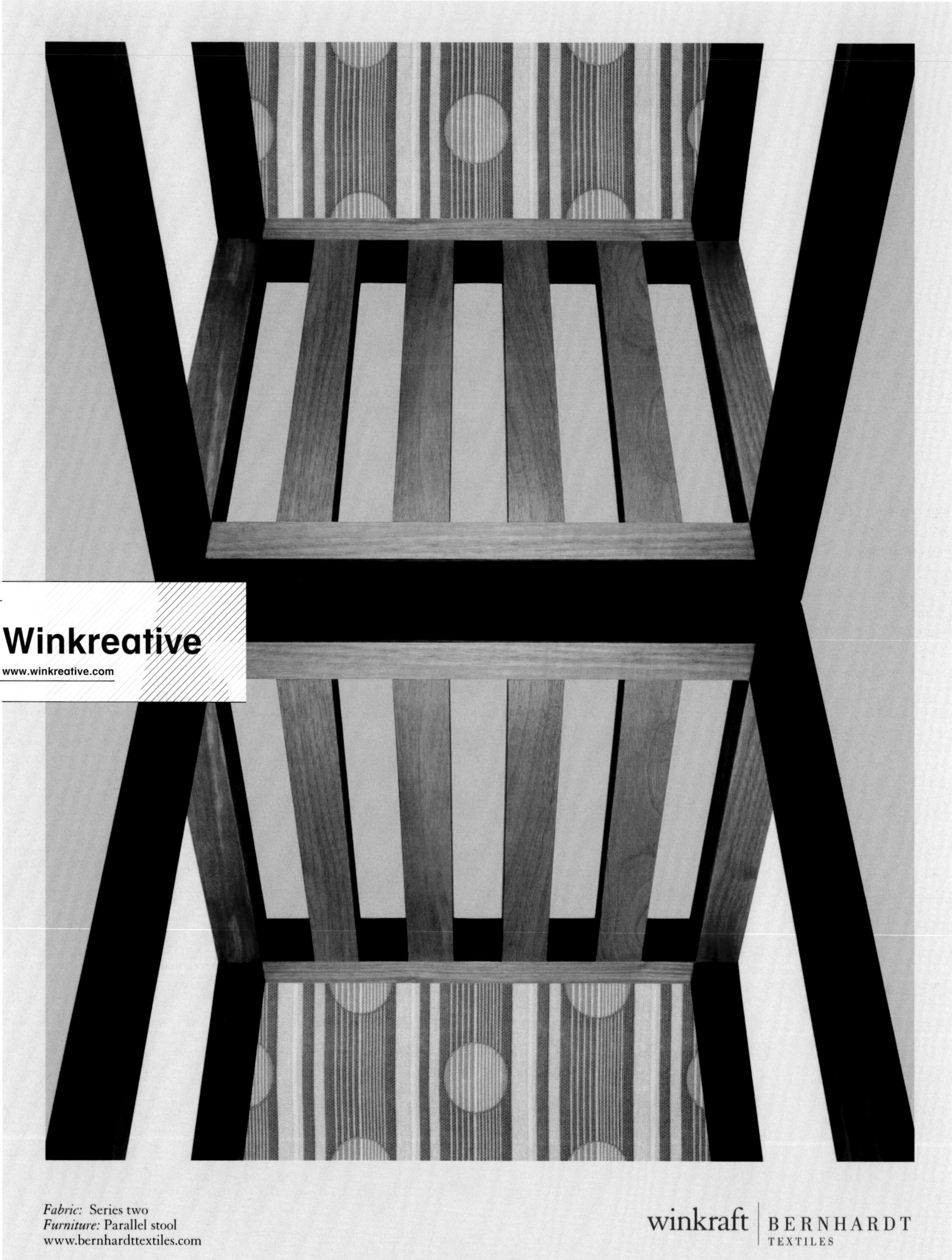

Fabric: Series two
Furniture: Parallel stool
www.bernhardttextiles.com

winkraft | BERNHARDT
TEXTILES

How did you start?

Winkreative was founded in 1998 by Tyler Brûlé. The business started as an editorially informed creative agency spun off from his magazine *Wallpaper**. The agency was launched in response to advertisers' demands for bespoke design, content and advertising solutions.

What is the background of the founders?

Tyler Brûlé started his career as a broadcast journalist for the BBC, until his passion for magazines took over in the form of *Wallpaper** and more recently *Monocle*. The commitment to quality editorial content together with branding and design knowhow produced Winkreative, which celebrated its ten-year anniversary in 2008.

What type of work do you mainly do?

Clients come from a wide variety of geographic locations and business sectors: from aviation, retail, finance, travel, technology and property development. Projects typically start with brand strategy and then move into creative direction combining graphic identity work, print and websites. Many clients come to us purely for our custom publication design and editorial expertise, however. Either way, an editorial viewpoint is placed at the centre of all projects in terms of content and design.

Where is your studio based, and why?

The headquarters for the business is in Zürich where all board decisions are made. The creative centre is in London, which works well for covering all time zones that we operate in – overlapping working days with Asia in the morning and the Americas in the afternoon and evening. We also find London helps us to put together an incredibly talented and international creative team. The Marylebone location of the office makes trips to Heathrow via Paddington convenient for both frequent outbound flights and incoming clients. We also have offices in New York and Tokyo so clients in those territories have relatively local account management contact.

Office opens at 7am. We have a handful of early starters with everyone in by 9.30am. Leaving time varies – 6pm is a luxury, necessity usually dictates a much later exit.

Do you have a place where you meet up after work?

Marylebone village is nice with plenty of options depending on the mood, but most often we'll open up the office fridge for post-work drinks with our colleagues at *Monocle* magazine.

How would you describe your studio?

Understated and functional – we're big proponents of well-made, quality products and we like to reflect that in our surroundings. There is plenty of woodwork by Swiss carpenters, divider screens designed by Japanese architects and low-level task lighting.

How many of you work there?

Around 60 in total in the building including rolling freelance requirements and *Monocle* magazine. We share space with the publication, so it's usually their culture editor who curates the iPod with whatever's new, or on the karaoke playlist.

WINKRAFT BRAND (AND CATALOGUE)
A COLLABORATION FURNITURE AND TEXTILE
MANUFACTURER BERNHARDT, FABRIC
COLLECTIONS INSPIRED BY URBAN LIVING
AND TRAVEL

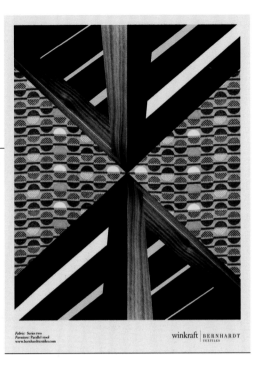

Where do you turn to for inspiration?

Between the agency and the magazine, the team does a lot of travelling so a vast amount of inspiration material reaches our desks from all over the world.

How would you say the design landscape has changed in the last 10 years?

More competition in terms of design, less competition in terms of quality content. Clients are more willing than ever to work across country borders and continents.

What would you say is the most distinctive characteristic of the visual arts in the UK?

A sense of freedom, personality and awareness.

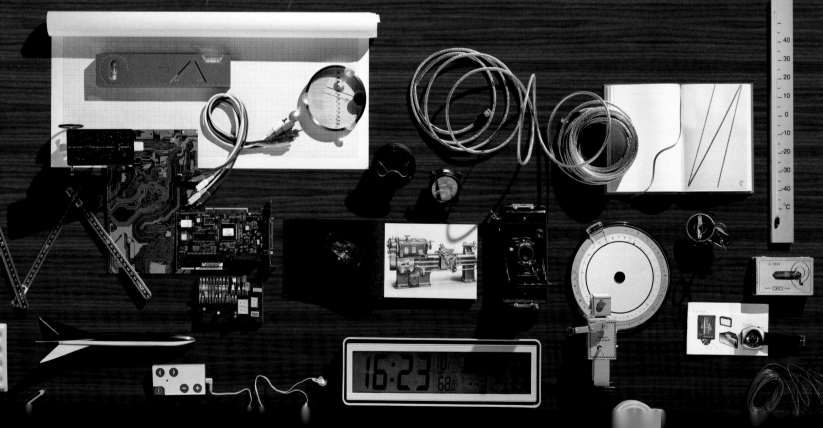

Wears:
Y & Kei, Adidas, BAPE
Worst fashion moment:
School uniform
Best fashion moment:
Being featured in *Sneaker Freaker* magazine
Inspired by:
Bathing Ape founder Nigo

HONG KONG

Michael Lee 26
Web Designer

Profiles

Wears:
Chloé, jeans all the time, vintage jewelry
Worst fashion moment:
Involved a gallery opening, a lot of red wine and beige cashmere
Best fashion moment:
Finding a 1940s Chanel brooch in the suburbs
Inspired by:
Coco Chanel

NEW YORK

Sophie Johnson 32
Art gallery receptionist

Profiles

Wears:
Isabela Capeto, Zara, jeans *du jour*
Worst fashion moment:
Breaking the heel of her silver sandals
Best fashion moment:
September issue of *Vogue* magazine
Inspired by:
Gisele Bündchen

SÃO PAULO

Maria-Helena Soares 27
History major at Universadade de São Paulo

Profiles

Wears:
Ralph Lauren, vintage sportswear, striped socks
Worst fashion moment:
The early '90s
Best fashion moment:
Discovering Comme des Garçons' London flagship
Inspired by:
Steve McQueen

LONDON

Pete Carter 28
Systems Analyst

Profiles

MAXÏMO PARK

OUR EARTHLY PLEASURES

YES

www.yesstudio.co.uk

MAXÏMO PARK "OUR EARTHLY PLEASURES" – ALBUM | WARP RECORDS | 2007

How did you start?
YES is a commercial art studio formed in 2004. Founding member Simon Earith was previously a creative director at influential 90s design agency Blue Source.

Who are your main clients, and what type of work do you mainly do?
We work for clients in many areas including; art, music, photography and broadcasting. Our output includes the design and art direction of books, record sleeves, identity and branding, printed matter, websites and title sequences.

Where is your studio based, and why?
We are based in a Victorian school in the East End of London, It's got a really nice canteen.

What's on your shelves? And on your walls?
We have a display shelf of second hand vinyl, and our pin-board charts our constantly growing collection of printed ephemera.

What kind of music do you play?
We play a pretty varied selection everything from Neil Young to Lindstrom & Prins Thomas.

How would you say the design landscape has changed in the last 10 years?
It's a shame the music industry is not the great commissioner of design it once was.

What would you say is the most distinctive characteristic of the visual arts in the UK?
Lots of massively talented smaller companies with a real sense of identity.

MAXĪMO PARK "GIRLS WHO PLAY GUITARS" – SINGLE
WARP RECORDS I 2007

WARP20
DESIGN & IDENTITY FOR 20TH ANNIVERSARY
CELEBRATION OF MUSIC LABEL WARP,
INCLUDING A SPECIAL EDITION BOX-SET

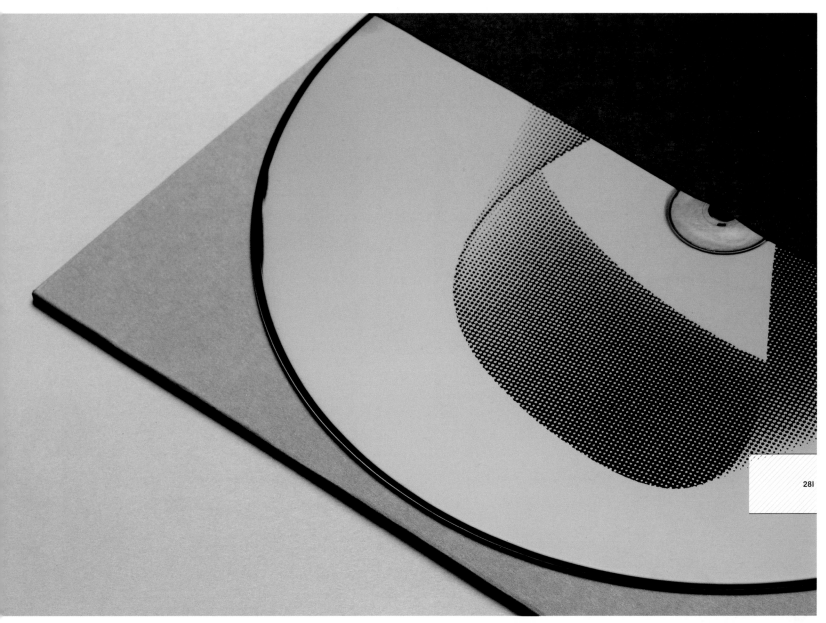